E. H. McCORMICK

New Zealand Literature

A SURVEY

LONDON
OXFORD UNIVERSITY PRESS
Wellington & Melbourne
1959

Oxford University Press, Amen House, London E.C.4
GLASGOW NEW YORK TORONTO MELBOURNE WELLINGTON
BOMBAY CALCUTTA MADRAS KARACHI KUALA LUMPUR
CAPE TOWN IBADAN NAIROBI ACCRA

© *Oxford University Press, 1959*

Printed in Great Britain

Contents

	Preface	vii
I	Before the Colonists	1
II	Colonial Beginnings	15
III	Seminal Years	21
IV	The Period of Expansion	40
V	The Nineties	69
VI	Years of Prosperity	82
VII	The Thirties	108
VIII	The Middle Decades	136
	References to Quotations	162
	Index	171

Preface

THE following survey is based on *Letters and Art in New Zealand* one of a series published by the New Zealand Government to mark the Centennial in 1940. In the present work the references to art have been omitted, the literary sections either revised or rewritten, and new material, amounting to almost one-third of the whole, introduced to carry the record up to the beginning of 1958. The plan of the book remains as before, but I have attempted to meet more exacting needs by substituting for the former note on sources specific references to quotations. I regret that limitations of space have allowed me to include only writers who have published at least one book. The rule has necessarily resulted in my ignoring accomplished writers, especially those of a younger generation. That injustice—with others—will doubtless be remedied in the comprehensive study of New Zealand letters which I hope some scholar will now be provoked into undertaking.

Though so belatedly, I should like to record my deep indebtedness in writing *Letters and Art* to Dr. Helen M. Simpson, the late Miss Ursula Bethell, and the late Sir Joseph Heenan. For help in preparing the present edition, my thanks are given to the staffs of several libraries, in particular the Library of the Auckland Institute and the Alexander Turnbull Library, Wellington. Acknowledgments are finally due to the New Zealand State Literary Fund for generously awarding me a scholarship to carry out this and other work.

AUCKLAND   E.H.M.
February 1958

I

Before the Colonists

THIS essay is chiefly concerned with the literature of New Zealand—more especially its imaginative literature—in the period of British occupation. Measured in terms of human history, that period is relatively brief. Little more than a century has passed since settlers of the New Zealand Company first met bleakness and disillusion as they landed at Port Nicholson; little more than a century since, in that warmer haven far to the north, the benign farce of Waitangi was enacted. Scarcely time for the migrant spirit to find a home, not long enough for an alien speech to shape itself to new surroundings: so it may seem as, from a distance, the critical historian surveys the work of his immediate ancestors and contemporaries.

But, comes the consoling reflection, this literature forms only part of his native inheritance. Long before it entered the European orbit, New Zealand was the home of 'writers'. There were poets in these islands when Chaucer was a youth; in the age of Shakespeare, an imaginative people had already built a local habitation for the myths and folk-tales of their distant homeland. Through the course of centuries, in an isolation unbroken, the Maoris created their own distinctive variation of Polynesian literature.

In this manner the literary genealogist of a new country may appease his hunger for age and duration and continuity. Nor need he desist here. The history of his own civilization in New Zealand is of some antiquity, reaching back as far as Milton's time. For nearly two centuries before 1840, the country was present—if remotely present—to the European mind. And the records of that era, more accessible than the 'literature' of the scriptless Maoris, serve in their turn to extend the New Zealand tradition beyond its brief colonial limits.

In the opening decades of the European era, records are, it must be confessed, of the meagrest. Details of the voyage to which New Zealand owed its name and, for a time, its forbidding reputation seeped slowly from Dutch sources. Not until 1671, long after Tasman's death, were his discoveries communicated to his countrymen in a brief narrative by Henrick Haelbos who had sailed with the expedition as ship's surgeon. An English rendering, issued the same year, told of a 'wild People' (the '*Southlanders*' Haelbos called them), 'gross of Body, undaunted, strong, and of a tawny colour', who, setting upon a boat's crew of the '*Hollanders*', slew four of their number. Because of his 'rough Entertainment', the narrative continues, Tasman named the anchorage '*Murderers-Bay*', and, sailing thence, reached 'a little Rocky Island', where the 'Inhabitants, a strong People, beckned to the Seamen'. Boats put out for water, but could not land 'by reason of the hollow Sea near the Shore'.[1]

It was thus, as one brief, ensanguined episode in a seventeenth-century traveller's tale, that the discovery of New Zealand came before the civilized world. Nor did later chronicles do much to retrieve the initial impression of an unfriendly people and an inhospitable shore. By 1682 there was circulating, in an English version, a description of the voyage compiled by a Dutch writer, van Nierop. Through the jejune phrases and nautical details of this '*short Relation out of the Journal of Captain* Abel Jansen Tasman' it is possible to discern some features of the country we know. On its first appearance it is described as 'very high and hilly' and elsewhere as 'a good Land, fruitful, and well scituated'; the contrariety and persistence of the winds are mentioned and the turbulence of the sea. The people, too, are rather more amply treated than in the naïve pages of Haelbos: they are 'rough of voice, thick and gross made', their colour 'between brown and yellow', their black hair 'bound fast and tight upon the crown of their head' and surmounted by 'a great thick white Feather'; one evening they played an instrument 'like a Moorish trumpet', on the Three Kings Island they carried 'sticks or clubs'. But here, as in Haelbos, the stress falls on that mysterious, motiveless incident in Murderers' Bay and on the country's harsh inaccessibility. The *Relation* concludes (it is told in the third person), 'upon *new Zealand* they had not so much as once been ashore.'²

Before the seventeenth century was out, the Dutch had founded the tradition of scholarship that was to culminate long after in J. E. Heeres's monumental edition of Tasman's *Journal* (1898). Not the compilation (1692) of Nicolaes Witsen nor the lavish folios (1724-6) of his successor, François Valentyn—not these but van Nierop's crabbed summary was the source from which European readers (even among the Dutch themselves) drew their knowledge of Tasman in the long period before navigators again visited the scene of his discoveries. Edited and paraphrased, translated and retranslated, reduced and amplified and recurtailed, the *Relation* pursued its career through eighteenth-century collections, perpetuating van Nierop's sombre picture of New Zealand and its pugnacious inhabitants. From his sparse particulars and the ambiguous line supplied by map-makers, theorists of rival nations spun their fantasies of wealth and dominion. It was insular, asserted one; it was a vast promontory, said another; some thought it was joined to New Holland, others (among them the Abbé Prévost) supposed it part of a separate continent at the antipodes of Europe. In the fertile imagination of Alexander Dalrymple, Tasman's landfall swelled to its greatest dimensions. He held that New Zealand was the western coast of a continent larger in extent than 'the whole civilized part of Asia, from Turkey eastward to the extremity of China'.³ The continent was somewhat sparsely peopled, for its inhabitants he later estimated at a meagre fifty millions.⁴

Then came Cook. 'This land,' wrote John Hawkesworth, describing the *Endeavour's* approach to New Zealand in the official account (1773) of the first expedition, 'This land became the subject of much eager conversation; but the general opinion seemed to be that we had found the *Terra australis incognita*.'⁵ So deeply had the myth of a Great Southern Continent penetrated the eighteenth-century mind, so intimately was its image fused with the hieroglyph bequeathed by Tasman to his successor. Cook dispelled the myth and solved the riddle of New Zealand's coastline. Drastically reduced in dimensions, the country took its place on the map as an inconspicuous group of islands set in windswept latitudes of the South Pacific.

Though failing to realize the larger territorial hopes, New Zealand nevertheless supplied abundant material for learned observation. The scientific gentlemen of Cook's entourage found it an untapped source of novel species and original phenomena which, duly recorded, found their way into successive accounts of the expeditions. These finely printed and illustrated volumes are not, however, mere compendia of organized and tabulated facts. Official publications and, even more notably, the unofficial, sometimes surreptitious literature that grew up round the three voyages gave scope for the play of the imagination and for that philosophic comment and surmise so dear to the eighteenth-century taste.

There was the rediscovered land itself, evoking from sentimental voyagers, even from the unemotional Cook (at least from his editors), enthusiastic superlatives. Of a village built on the summit of a much-admired perforated rock, Hawkesworth remarks, 'the situation . . . was the most beautifully romantic that can be imagined. . . .'[6] In his *Journal* (1773) the young Sydney Parkinson also exclaims at the 'romantic' appearance of the land, with 'mountains piled on mountains to an amazing height', and elsewhere writes, 'The country about the bay is agreeable beyond description. . . .'[7] George Forster's *Voyage round the World* (1777) verbosely echoes the same sentiments, 'The grandeur of this scene was such, that the powers of description fall short of the force and beauty of nature. . . .'[8] In only one respect was the country deficient—the complaint recurs—in its lack of civilization. To his comment on the mountains Parkinson adds, 'but they seemed to be uninhabited', and to his description of the bay, 'with proper cultivation, it might be rendered a kind of second Paradise.'[9] Forster, again, turns from inanimate nature to contemplate the changes effected by the expedition in a brief stay ashore —the clearing of forest, the recording of 'animals and vegetables', the setting up of a forge and an observatory. 'In a word,' he concludes the catalogue, 'all around us we perceived the rise of arts, and the dawn of science, in a country which had hitherto lain plunged in one long night of ignorance and barbarism!'[10]

And the people, the 'Indians', were they included in this gloomy generalization? Forster thought so, but his uncompromising view was contradicted—at any rate modified—by other writers. Warlike the natives were on a first meeting, intractable, bold to a troublesome degree, and, as Parkinson and Hawkesworth both noted, outwardly less attractive than the Tahitians— not equal to them in 'personal delicacy', 'ruder' in address, and altogether 'more unpolished'.[11] In addition, evidence of the horrid fact gradually emerged: beyond all possibility of doubt, the denizens of this potential paradise were anthropophagi, eaters of human flesh, cannibals!

All this—and more—could be counted on the debit side, as contemplative voyagers reckoned up the balance-sheet of savage life. On the other hand, these barbarous islanders proved on closer acquaintance less intimidating than they seemed at first sight: they exhibited parental love, grief for the dead, loyalty to one another; they could be kindly, courteous, affectionate—they were human. To victims of an enforced and uncongenial celibacy, moreover, they represented a source of feminine consolation, not exclusively physical and not always venal. John Rickman, author of a surreptitious *Journal* (1781), recounts the story of a tender attachment between a young sailor and a Maori girl, commenting finally that, outside the pages of romance, such love was unknown 'in those enlightened countries, where the boasted refinements of sentiment have circumscribed the purity of affection and narrowed it away to mere conjugal fidelity.'[12]

Cannibalism itself, if not condoned, could be temperately studied and, in its turn, used to demonstrate the failings of European society. 'But though we are too much polished to be cannibals,' wrote Forster, 'we do not find it unnaturally and savagely cruel to take the field, and to cut one another's throats by thousands, without a single motive, besides the ambition of a prince, or the caprice of his mistress!'[13] The republican sentiment of this passage would, one supposes, have been offensive to Cook, but not its humanity. His own consideration of the same custom in the official account (1777) of the second voyage was, in fact, the occasion for a sympathetic appraisal of the people and their condition: 'The New Zealanders are certainly in some state of civilization; their behaviour to us was manly and mild, shewing, on all occasions, a readiness to oblige. They have some arts among them which they execute with great judgment, and unwearied patience; they are less addicted to thieving than the other islanders of the South Sea; and, I believe, those in the same tribe, or such as are at peace one with another, are strictly honest among themselves.' As for cannibalism, it was an ancient practice which had persisted in New Zealand, he believed, because of the country's isolation and the consequent lack of 'commerce with strangers', chief civilizing agency of the human race. 'An intercourse with foreigners,' he advised, 'would reform their manners, and polish their savage minds.' [14]

It is the eighteenth-century prescription, offered in varying terminology and with varying emphasis, throughout the collection. Only by the example of enlightened mentors, only through the introduction of civilized arts and amenities, would the country and the people be redeemed from their state of barbarism or semi-barbarism. Yet Cook himself records with disapproval one consequence of civilization as it had spread ashore from the *Adventure* and the *Discovery*. In describing the 'shameful traffic' in native women which grew up during the second voyage (the darker aspect of Rickman's touching idyll), he wrote, 'During our stay in the Sound, I had observed that this second visit made to this country, had not mended the morals of the natives of either sex.' [15] Hence the rediscoverer of New Zealand is an early witness to the twofold effects of that civilizing process of which he was perhaps the most powerful single agent.

Cook, like Tasman before him, waited long for the supreme tribute of exacting scholarship. Only in our own day, through the exegetic ardour of his New Zealand editor, J. C. Beaglehole, is the pure text of his utterance being freed from the additions of eighteenth-century amplifiers and improvers. When completed, the magnificent new series of Cook's *Journals* (1955–) will provide a record of the expeditions unique in fullness and authenticity. It will not, however, relegate Hawkesworth,

Parkinson, and the rest to the limbo of useless and forgotten things. With their elegant bindings and finely engraved plates, they will always have a place on the shelves of the collector; and the literary antiquarian, borne on the stream of their measured prose, will continue to reflect that these volumes numbered Samuel Johnson among their original public, that they stood in the libraries of Jane Austen's country-houses, that they fed the mind and imagination of the youthful Coleridge.

The young Chateaubriand was less well served by the navigators of his nation. French voyages to the South Pacific in the late eighteenth century were imperfectly recorded, and the accounts, such as they were, supplied little to inspire the flight of romantic pinions. The first small work to describe French experience of New Zealand was concerned with an affray far bloodier and apparently even more treacherous than the murder of Tasman's men in the previous century. The *Nouveau Voyage à la Mer du Sud* (1783) recounts the slaughter of Marion du Fresne and his crew on a voyage charitably promoted to restore to his home a Tahitian whom Bougainville had brought to Europe as a human curiosity. To read this book is to realize anew how bitter was the debate between the followers of Rousseau and the supporters of the old order in France. This was a test case. Here was natural man living in perfect surroundings, untouched by the influence of civilization. Was he as virtuous as philosophers claimed? At the outset, so it appeared. The French voyagers seemed to have discovered the most kindly and humane, the most hospitable people on earth. Had they left soon after their arrival, reflects the author, Crozet, philosophers given to the praise of primitive man would have been overjoyed to see their bookish theorizings confirmed by first-hand accounts. Primitive man, as the massacre proved, was treacherous, blood-thirsty, cruel. After relating the details of that mysterious incident, Crozet cannot resist gloating over the discomfiture of the *philosophes* who, knowing nothing of savage people, idealized them at the expense of those whom they were pleased to call 'artificial', merely 'because education has improved their minds!'[16]

Eighteenth-century New Zealand thus formed a debating

ground for the clash of ideas which, a few years later, was to culminate in the French Revolution. Nor are the sentiments of the book always in favour of the *ancien régime*. In certain passages, especially where the hand of its editor, Alexis Rochon, is noticeable, there is a clear expression of the revolutionary principles of equality and fraternity. Crozet records that the expedition took possession of the 'island of New Zealand' in the name of the King, but Rochon writes, 'We forget that the land where these savages live belongs to them quite as much as our own land does to us.' Elsewhere he reckons up the benefits conferred by these voyages, 'so much glorified by Europeans', concluding that the few useful animals, the few seeds left by travellers, were but poor compensation for the crimes, always avenged by fresh crimes, for the evil done to the natives, and for the contagion spread amongst them.[17]

Marion's fate doubtless coloured the expectations and so the impressions of his immediate successors. For example, in the *Voyage de Dentrecasteaux* (1808) the Maoris, glimpsed during a brief visit, are described as 'sombre and fierce'; and in another passage the narrator describes the 'horror' with which the voyagers recognized human bones in a necklace worn by one of the natives.[18] Happily, this picture of a savage and perfidious race did not remain unmodified in the literature of French exploration; it was amended and amplified by the writings of Dumont d'Urville, recently made accessible to New Zealand readers in two works by Olive Wright, *New Zealand 1826–1827* (1950) and *The Voyage of the 'Astrolabe'—1840* (1955). These admirable volumes, presenting the narratives of d'Urville's two major expeditions to New Zealand, are, among the records of the navigators, second only to Cook's in breadth of scope and historical interest.

Dumont d'Urville was that rarest of men, combining in his person with complete harmony the qualities of scholar and man of action. Linguist, classical student, botanist of distinction, he also belongs in the company of great captains and navigators, falling short of the greatest, it may be, only because the date of his birth circumscribed his opportunities. To the New Zealand reader not the least of his recommendations is his regard for this country and his interest in its past; indeed, he must have been the first European to conceive the idea of a New Zealand tradition. In the *Voyage de la Corvette l'Astrolabe* (1830-5) he describes the joyful expectations with which the expedition saw before them these wild coasts and towering mountains, swept by winds from the Antarctic. Here (to paraphrase and curtail his eloquence), each man felt, as he proudly followed in the path of Tasman, of Cook, of Marion, was a theatre worthy of his researches. And d'Urville's imagination reached back far beyond historic, beyond human times; in a striking passage he describes his feelings as he walked through the forest at midday, when even the sound of birds was stilled: 'Passing through these mournful solitudes, one might think oneself transported to that age when nature, having brought forth the beings of the vegetable kingdom, still awaited the decrees of the eternal power to bring to life the animal kind.' Later, in nineteenth-century manner, he is peering into a future when flourishing cities will stand on coasts now deserted or peopled only by isolated *pas*; when ships of every size will plough through now-silent waters; when the academicians of New Zealand will question, or at least laboriously discuss, the narratives of the earliest navigators.[19]

D'Urville brought to the study of New Zealand not only his powers as an imaginative writer and his European sense of the past but also gifts as historian and man of science. Under his editorship was published a collection of the 'Chronicles of New Zealand', a comprehensive source-book, compiled, he explains, for the benefit of 'those who choose to study the human race in the childhood of civilization'.[20] He himself viewed the 'children' of a prehistoric era with the scholar's interest and, ultimately, with compassion; in the account of his final expedition, the *Voyage au Pole Sud* (1842-54), he noted with sorrow that the native virtues he had admired on his earlier visits were fast disappearing: in the neighbourhood of the whaling-stations, at least, a nation of independent warriors had been reduced to a motley tribe of mendicants clothed in rags.[21] The last of the navigators thus testified to changes, some good, many evil, for which he and his predecessors had involuntarily opened the way. With the passing of the ancient Maori mode of life, Dumont d'Urville saw the close of one phase in New Zealand history; and in May 1840, as he sailed from the Bay of Islands, he left behind him a country now under British rule, its future irrevocably linked with a distant and alien civilization.

The seventy years or so that separate Cook's first visit from the final expedition of d'Urville saw the gradual infiltration of Europeans following in the wake of the navigators. In the narratives of later voyages there is frequent mention of these precursors of settlement—whalers, traders, missionaries, and others less reputable. But they possess a small literature of their own which bridges the gap between discovery and active colonization.

There is a uniformity in the contents of these successive *Narratives* and *Journals* such as one finds in the Victorian literature of Darkest Africa or in the Central Asian travel-books of more recent times. Most authors supplied a liberal portion of sensation; it might be an authentic description of a cannibal feast, or a verbatim account, drawn from the chief actors, of the *Boyd* massacre, or a blood-curdling narrative of ritual murder. A description of tattooing, the procedure and the finished process, is generally given, and invariably a picture of the quaint ceremonies of greeting and farewell. Houses, habits and morals, implements, canoes, dress—all are recorded with varying degrees of accuracy, while the more venturesome authors penetrate into the speculative regions of religion and mythology. A résumé of New Zealand history is often supplied and a vocabulary of the Language of the New Zealanders rendered with all the eccentricity of writers capable of such examples of transliteration as 'Narpooes', 'E. O. Ke-Angha', 'Kiddy-Kiddy', or—prize grotesque—'Too-gee Te-ter-re-nu-e Warri-pe-do'. Finally comes a survey of the country's potential wealth and opinions, always favourable, about its suitability for European colonization.

In their approach to this common material the authors showed great differences, as might be expected from the varying motives that drew men to this wild and distant country. The modest and sketchy *Account* (1807) of Dr. John Savage and Captain Richard Cruise's *Journal* (1823) were both incidental products of expeditions despatched from the colony of New South Wales, and neither is very far removed from the day-to-day journal of conscientious officialdom. Savage, agreeably surprised on his arrival to find that a race of notorious cannibals betrayed 'no symptom of savage ferocity', decided on closer acquaintance that these 'Indians' were 'of a very superior order, both in point of personal appearance and intellectual endowments'—a conclusion supported by his study of 'Moyhanger', a native taken by him to England to be exhibited in Courts and drawing-rooms as a specimen of natural man.[22] In the years that elapsed between Savage and Cruise the Maoris had become only too familiar to vagrant Europeans as a source of labour for visiting ships and as partners in a wholesale commerce whose modest beginnings had been noted by Cook. Cruise's *Journal* has at least the merit of explicitness; there is a whole volume on the relations between Europeans and Maoris packed into an entry like this: 'The biscuit had been a part of their ration for many months, but in consequence of the incalculable quantity of vermin contained in it, had become perfectly useless, except as an article of barter with the natives....'[23]

Ampler and more illuminating is the *Narrative* (1817) of John Liddiard Nicholas who, in 1814, accompanied Samuel Marsden on his first visit to New Zealand. When reading Nicholas we are again transported to a world of eighteenth-century ideas and modes of expression. With leisurely magniloquence he unfolds the story of that memorable visit, interspersing his narrative with moral reflections and philosophizings like those which adorn the pages of Hawkesworth and Forster. In spite of his own religious orthodoxy, in spite of the *Boyd* massacre and atrocities enacted before his eyes, Nicholas was still inclined to wonder whether the 'wayward philosopher of Geneva' might not, after all, be right in his opinion that 'the best and kindest affections of the human heart are found only in the man who has neither been born amidst the luxuries, nor educated in the refinements of civilized society.' But that momentary feeling was brushed aside, and Nicholas left New Zealand convinced that the true genius of its people would be elicited only when they were introduced to 'the various pursuits of culture and civilization.'[24]

Except for his fleeting dalliance with Rousseauism, Nicholas was in every respect a fitting chronicler of Marsden; and until the missionary's scattered writings were collected by J. R. Elder more than a century later, the *Narrative* contained the fullest accessible account of the historic first visit to the Bay of Islands. The evangelist of early New Zealand was also rooted in the eighteenth century, and though he expressed himself in less ornate fashion than Nicholas, his writings, like his religious views, bear upon them the unmistakable imprint of the age of reason. We are reminded of Cook when, in one of his numerous eulogies, he writes of the Maoris, 'I do not believe that there is in any part of the world, or ever was, a native in a state of nature superior to the inhabitants of New Zealand . . . nor anywhere people who would in a shorter period render themselves worthy of being numbered with civilized nations, provided they were favoured with the ordinary means of instruction in these civil arts by which men are gradually refined and polished.' Again, in a judicious consideration of cannibalism he is reminiscent of Forster: 'As far as I can form an opinion of this horrid custom, I am inclined to believe that the New Zealanders do not consider it any more crime to eat their enemies than civilized nations do to hang an offender, although at the same time it stamps as much public disgrace upon the surviving relatives as the public execution of a criminal in Europe reflects upon the family of the sufferer.'[25]

The close-packed pages of his *Letters and Journals* (1932) demonstrate that Marsden was a writer of more than ordinary distinction. There is no conscious striving for literary effect—such artifices he would have scorned as instruments of the Prince of Darkness—but the earnest, simple narrative, relieved here and there by a metaphor of scriptural beauty and aptness, is as dramatic and effective as the most skilfully contrived work of literary art. Every stage of the drama is presented: the early resolution to free the Maoris from their 'cruel spiritual bondage'; the obstacles and delays so numerous and persistent that they would have deterred less resolute a character; the ultimate establishment of the mission, despite the fact that no clergyman would venture to a country where 'he could anticipate nothing less than to be killed and eaten by the natives'; the heart-breaking lapses of the missionaries themselves; then, at length, in salvaged souls and cultivated fields, certain evidence that the enterprise had not been vainly undertaken.[26]

It is a comment on the contradictions and antagonisms in the small European society of pre-colonial New Zealand that the man who stands next to Marsden in the hierarchy of writers (though far below him) presents the least favourable view of the missionaries. In his *Narrative of a Nine Months' Residence* (1832) Augustus Earle never loses an opportunity of castigating 'these pious men', 'these comfortable teachers of the Gospel,' as he terms them, whether for their grudging charity, or their self-righteousness, or, worst of crimes, for obscuring the 'finest human forms' under clumsy European clothing. For Earle was an artist and viewed the Maoris rather as subjects for sketch and painting than as souls to be retrieved from the dominion of Satan. He describes the beauty of their naked forms, the picturesque disposition of their forces as they landed from their war-canoes or greeted a visiting party, and their respect for the fine arts, shown in the honour paid to the expert tattooer, 'Aranghie', whose 'heads', he remarks, were as much prized in New Zealand as Sir Thomas Lawrence's in Britain. Like artists before and since his time, Earle saw the Maoris as beings of an earlier heroic age— a conception that is beautifully conveyed in his painting, 'The Wounded Chief Honghi and his Family,' now in the Alexander Turnbull Library. 'To me,' he wrote of the scene, 'it almost seemed to realize some of the passages of Homer. . . .'[27] But he was no romantic, and having no theoretical or doctrinal axe to grind, he saw not only the heroic side of the people but also the brutality, the license, and the insecurity of that state intermediate between the truly primitive and the civilized. Earle was a tolerant, kindly man, blessed with imagination and a sense of humour—

qualities that went into the least pretentious and most delightful book on early New Zealand.

Joel Samuel Polack would, one supposes, have guffawed loudly at the suggestion that Hongi in any way resembled the heroes of the *Odyssey*. With all the assurance of the 'man who knows', he would have dismissed Earle as a mere tourist, a mayfly, while he, J. S. Polack, with six years' experience behind him—then would have followed a flood of lively reminiscences, filled with hair-raising anecdotes, execrable puns, and malapropisms. He is a picturesque and astonishingly versatile figure, this early storekeeper-trader-artist-author, with all the blustering self-confidence that was, he implies, needed for the hazardous pursuit of commerce in the eighteen-thirties. His two-volume *New Zealand: Being a Narrative of Travels and Adventures* (1838) is an entertaining cyclopedia of New Zealand culled from the most varied sources, written and oral. It recounts the history of New Zealand, beginning with the European discovery of the Pacific; it describes Polack's own personal experience of the Maoris; it minutely defines and explains the habits of that people; it relates the grievances of European traders; finally, it cajoles, implores, and commands Great Britain to colonize the islands. Great Britain was to respond, but with considerable reluctance; and, after spending some years abroad, Polack returned to New Zealand in the early forties, doubtless confirmed in the opinion that largely by his efforts the country had been made safe for settlement—and trade.

II

Colonial Beginnings

So much, then, for the forerunners of the New Zealand writer —the Maori poet, emerging dimly from antique times; the European voyagers of the seventeenth, eighteenth, and early nineteenth centuries, now elevated to a stature almost legendary; the saints and sages and swashbucklers who dared to visit, even to inhabit a New Zealand notorious as the Alsatia of the Pacific. These men, through their works, have a continuous vitality; their heirs are those who care to seek them out in libraries and collections. The fact is, however, that modern New Zealand derives in the direct line not from the culture of the primitive Maori, nor from the spacious civilization of the eighteenth century, nor from the discordant elements of pre-colonization days, but from an age not yet distant enough to be glamorous. Its immediate origins go back only to early Victorian times.

Yet to the prosperous Englishman of the eighteen-forties and early fifties it might well have seemed that no colony, unless perhaps Virginia, had been founded in a more auspicious age. With the French menace finally quelled at Waterloo, Britain had settled to thirty years and more of peace and security. She had freed her slaves, she had enfranchised her own people—or all that could, with safety, be enfranchised. And as proof that virtue brings its reward even in material things, her prosperity had increased to a gratifying degree. Now the manufactory of the world, she poured goods, men, money, ships into every quarter— and with them her language, her theories of government, her religious ideas, her humanitarianism.

Nor, in spite of her Continental critics with their 'nation of shopkeepers' gibe, was early Victorian Britain lacking in literary achievement. True, the romantic writers were dead, or silent, or

—witness the aged Thomas Campbell with his 'Song' for the New Zealand emigrants:

> *Steer, helmsman, till you steer our way,*
>   *By stars beyond the line;*
> *We go to found a realm, one day,*
>   *Like England's self to shine.*[1]

—feebly echoing the tunes of their youth. But a new generation of writers had grown up; and, as an emigrant to the Canterbury Settlement in the early fifties packed his collection of contemporary classics, he would have found it difficult not to exceed the space that could be reasonably set aside for the luxury of books.

Such a man would almost certainly have placed in his trunks an assortment of verse, for in Victorian England the profession of poetry was widely esteemed and sometimes lucrative. There were, first, the works of Mr. Tennyson—*Poems*, *The Princess* (that topical poem on the woman question), and now just off the press, *In Memoriam*, a work to be pondered over in private during the voyage, read aloud in the family circle, and later memorized in parts and transcribed into the reader's commonplace-book. Mr. and Mrs. Browning would have been included, Mrs. Browning for even stronger reasons than her husband, ranging as she did from 'The Cry of the Children' to the *Sonnets from the Portuguese*. A discriminating emigrant might have taken to the colony *The Strayed Reveller* by 'A' (said to be Matthew Arnold, son of the headmaster of Rugby), or a copy of *The Germ*, a magazine brought out by a group of young men who called themselves the 'Pre-Raphaelite Brotherhood' and preached startling doctrines of art and poetry.

A university man might very well have decided to bring with him a copy of Clough's *Bothie of Tober-na-Vuolich* with its playful references to such a visionary emigrant as himself:

> *They are married and gone to New Zealand.*
> *Five hundred pounds in pocket, with books, and two or three pictures,*
> *Tool-box, plough, and the rest, they rounded the sphere to New*
>   *Zealand.*
> *There he hewed, and dug; subdued the earth and his spirit....*[2]

Or he might have slipped into some vacant corner a slight volume, *Venice*, by Alfred Domett, now well established as a settler in New Zealand. Mr. Domett, it would seem from this long reflective poem, had seen in the decay of Venice a sign of Europe's ultimate fate, then, turning to 'tracts yet rough with nature', had beheld the vision of a brighter future:

> *There lurks the raw material of Renown!*
> *There Genius yet shall dare the perilous verge*
> *Of passionate Thought—some Bacon there hurl down*
> *The tide of mind to channels new....*[3]

When it came to selecting works of prose, the emigrant's problem would have been one of infinite difficulty. In spite of their bulk, he would have been reluctant to leave behind any of the novels of Charles Dickens who, since emigration was now in the air, in winding up *David Copperfield*, had just despatched the Micawber family to the antipodes. Then there was *Vanity Fair*, Thackeray's masterpiece completed at last only to be overshadowed by that amazing novel, *Jane Eyre*—the work, it now appeared, not of a man but of a female writer, Charlotte Brontë. If *Jane Eyre* were debarred from the family circle, there was a plenitude of fireside reading in the works of Captain Marryat, of Bulwer, of Lever, of Charles Kingsley. Thinking of long winter nights in the colony, the emigrant would pack *Peter Simple*, *The Last of the Barons*, *Charles O'Malley*, *Alton Locke*, and many three-volume favourites.

Essential to the library of both the educated settler and the ambitious mechanic would have been a bulky section of serious and improving works. There were the *Critical and Historical Essays* of Macaulay, indispensable on any Victorian bookshelf, and, to contrast with Macaulay's complacent rhetoric, the *Chartism* and *Past and Present* of Carlyle. More than likely John Stuart Mill's *Political Economy* would have found its way into the luggage of many settlers who left after 1848, and it is not inconceivable that some radical emigrant took with him the *Communist Manifesto*. (For the age of prosperity and expansion saw the creation of a vast proletariat; it produced not only

'God's in His Heaven' but 'The Song of the Shirt'.) Finally—since the emigrant's trunk is already full to bursting—some works on the great religious questions of the day would certainly have been included; not till later was the impact of Darwinism felt, but the Tractarian controversy raged bitterly and many copies of *Tracts for the Times* must have been imported to the colony and, in particular, to the Puseyite Canterbury settlement.

These were a few of the seeds of New Zealand literature that might have been introduced by such a settler as James Edward FitzGerald; FitzGerald, indeed, the associate and correspondent of Ruskin, of Charles Kingsley, of Gladstone, may be taken as representative of the men of talent who, bringing with them the ideas and ideals of nineteenth-century Britain, did so much to shape the early years of the colony and, to some extent, its later development. Irish by blood, English by education, grandson of a baronet, graduate of Cambridge, he belonged to a family of soldiers and administrators. As Under-secretary at the British Museum, he had seen the rebuilding of that monument to Victorian enlightenment, and he may have discussed with Panizzi plans for its crowning-piece, the great domed reading-room. He would have seen the Palace of Westminster as it slowly took shape, perhaps giving rise in his mind to the Canterbury provincial buildings later to be built in modest emulation. With mingled feelings on the point of embarkation, he would have read or heard the 'Poetical Offering' of Martin Tupper who, looking with seer's eye on a dubious future, had been reassured by the departure of the Canterbury pilgrims:

> *Even should Britain's decay be down-written*
> *In the dread doom-book that no man may search,*
> *Still shall an Oxford, a London, a Britain,*
> *Gladden the South with a Home and a Church!*[4]

A poet himself, FitzGerald had made his own contribution to the nascent literature of New Zealand in the 'Night-watch Song of the *Charlotte Jane*'. Here, in his invocation to 'the fathers of our line', is a sample:

> *Though their tombs may not receive us,*
> *Far o'er the ocean blue,*
> *Their spirits ne'er shall leave us,*
> *In the land we are going to.*[5]

In this one man are illustrated the contradictions, the virtues, the strength, and some of the weaknesses of New Zealand's founders. He left a responsible post and the prospect of worldly advancement to pursue an ideal to the other side of the earth. Genuinely believing that a new and better society might be created, he urged the legislators of Canterbury to remember their freedom from 'the principles, the sentiments, and the traditions' of Britain,[6] only to be reproached in later years by Sir George Grey for 'striving to transport the old world in portions to the new'.[7] In political assemblies noted for their oratory he won fame as a speaker—fluent, eloquent, though to the modern taste sometimes over-rhetorical. He led a busy life as administrator and civil servant, yet found time for the writing of prose articles that are newspaper journalism only because the colony provided facilities for little else. As versifier, his quality may be fairly measured by the 'Night-watch Song'. Despite a certain sad poignancy and the interest it has acquired from old associations, the poem is irretrievably dead. Its phrases—'the fathers of our line', 'far o'er the ocean blue', 'sweet smiles from eyes of blue'— were the tarnished currency of a tradition already outworn. In short, the occasion was worthy of a poet, and FitzGerald, like Tupper, was only a poetaster.

It was in this way and by men like this that the next phase of New Zealand history was begun. FitzGerald, Domett, the Wakefields, Grey—as we look back at them over a century or so, it is impossible to withhold our respect, albeit a modified respect. We may admire their courage and their high seriousness of purpose, flawed though they seem in the cold forms of print with the Victorian vice of cant. We may enjoy their prose writings, whether in the journals and letters they wrote with such charm and assiduity, or in their full-dress performances in books, periodicals, newspapers, even in official files and reports. If our approval of their more ambitious efforts in the Gothic manner must be qualified, we can still look with pleasure on their first unpretentious buildings. With few exceptions, we can only deplore the badness of their verses and that habit of slack poeticizing which they transmitted to their colonial posterity.

When the accounts are cast, the founders of New Zealand are seen to have done very well by their adopted country. But, impatient at the shortness of their lineage and yearning for the fulfilment of a colonial New England, their descendants are sometimes heard to complain unreasonably, 'Would they had come a century or two earlier!'

III

Seminal Years

'WOULD they had come a century or two earlier' to prepare the way in the mid-nineteenth century for a New Zealand Hawthorne and his drama of Calvinist frustration set, it would be fitting, in the stern hinterland of Otago; for a Melville to interpret those sordid, picturesque, ennobling, barbarous decades in the Bay of Islands; for an Emerson to weave his philosophy in the cloisters of Canterbury, or a Thoreau to muse and write— again it would be fitting—on the lakeside at Tutira. . . . The dreams dissolve, and we are left with—what? Nothing remotely comparable with the flowering of New England, it is true, but with a miscellany of prose and verse that is not discreditable to its authors, given the circumstances.

The circumstances—how large and how limiting a part they have in New Zealand's early years as a British colony! In six small settlements were gathered a few thousand people drawn from every quarter of the British Isles and set down, often with scant preparation, in surroundings whose very grandeur held the promise of isolation, physical danger, and hard toil. There were forests to clear, homes to build, farms to break in, exploration and surveying to be undertaken; a native people to be understood and conciliated; constitutions, regulations, laws—all the machinery of men in society—to be fashioned and applied. Then there were painful adjustments to be made by people, some of them deluded seekers after the New Jerusalem, who were forced into a new and utterly uncongenial way of life. Can we wonder that there was no great efflorescence of literature in these foundation years? The real question is how so much, relatively, came to be produced.

For there is another side to this picture of struggle and privation. Granted that the 'six colonies of New Zealand' were small and isolated; yet they were in a real sense communities—associations of people welded together into some sort of whole by a common origin, by common aims, and often, it must be admitted, by common grievances. 'We are,' runs the manifesto of an early periodical, 'a community of brethren, having common objects in view—to reclaim and occupy the waste places of this land . . . to cultivate the arts and sciences, and the practice and extension of the amenities of civilized life.'[1] In nostalgic moments one wonders whether so positive a statement could have been made in any later period of history; whether, in fact, Port Nicholson and Nelson and Dunedin in their early years were not, apart from the centres of ancient Maori life, the first and last genuine communities in this country. What is clear is that the New Zealand of Domett, FitzGerald, Grey, and Barr did provide some of the necessary conditions for the writer—an interested audience, a sense of direction, and, in a new country and a new people, an inexhaustible theme.

Nor must the liberal role of the New Zealand Company be forgotten. The Company, so often reviled by the immigrants and their posterity, was after all instrumental in forming *settlements*; this much was salvaged from the wreck of the Wakefield scheme, that immigrants were encouraged to gather in groups rather than disperse themselves and so risk the barbarizing effects of isolation. It was the Company, too, that brought here many of the writers, either as settlers or employees. In spite of its errors and sins, for more than a decade and especially in its early prosperous years, it acted as a generous patron, organizing expeditions into the interior, encouraging its servants to record what they saw, publishing the results in handsome books and lavish folios.

For these reasons it is fitting that a book produced under the Company's auspices and written by the son of Edward Gibbon Wakefield should give the fullest and most illuminating account of the first years of settlement. Edward Jerningham Wakefield saw the foundation of New Zealand from the turning of the first sod. While still a boy of nineteen and attracted, as he says, by the prospects of 'novelty and adventure' in the new colony, he joined the *Tory* expedition which left England in 1839. His intention had been to wait only for the landing of the first settlers, after which he was to embark on one of the returning emigrant ships; but he explains, 'So interesting . . . did it become to watch the first steps of the infant colony, and so exciting to march among the ranks of its hardy founders, that I was tempted to postpone my return for four years after their arrival.'[2] The experience of these years he set down in *Adventure in New Zealand* (1845).

The contents of the book do not belie the title; here is the troubled surface of New Zealand life in the transition period between No Man's Land and colony described in all its romantic variety. As secretary to his uncle, Colonel William Wakefield, and later as explorer and negotiator in his own right, Jerningham had unique opportunities for seeing at first hand the events of that exciting and sometimes ominous chapter in our history. He met the Cook Strait whalers, with their rigid professional code, their picturesque dress, and their equally picturesque argot— 'grunters' for pigs, 'spuds' for potatoes, 'spreaders' for blankets, 'squeakers' for children; he saw flax-dressers at work and carefully described their elaborate technique; he met missionaries of various persuasions and varying degrees of piety—one whose manners were 'conciliating, and essentially those of a gentleman and man of the world', a second bluntly labelled 'land-shark', a third, the saintly Octavius Hadfield, characterized by the profane whalers of Kapiti as 'a missionary, but . . . a gentleman every inch of him'; he saw and described Maoris of every sort and condition from Te Puni, 'a gentleman in every sense of the word' (Wakefield's highest and ever-recurring term of praise) to the noisily arrogant Rangihaeata and Karitahi, clad in 'an old dragoon helmet, and black tail-coat without trousers'.[3]

Wakefield had a novelist's eye for detail, shown when, with malicious intent, he describes the ridiculous ceremony of striking the flag over the 'snoring grog-shops' on the beach at Thorndon, while 'two or three people in their night-caps' peeped from doors and windows.[4] He had, too, a Victorian novelist's habit of grouping his characters into blacks and whites, villains and heroes, the villains usually being the opponents of the Company, the heroes its friends. And when dilating, sometimes at tedious length, on the squabbles between Government and Company, he had a novelist's disregard for fact. But we do not today need to go to Wakefield for facts; these have since been recorded by more mature and more objective historians. We can read him for the glimpses he provides of the manners and morals of our great-grandfathers, for his record of fashions in dress and speech long since vanished, for his descriptions of a people and a country still retaining some of their primitive innocence, and for his narrative of journeys and adventures set down with all the youthful gusto he brought to those experiences.

Gusto is not a word one would use in describing the *Travels in New Zealand* (1843) of Ernest Dieffenbach who came with Wakefield as the naturalist and surgeon of the expedition; indeed, similar experiences can rarely have been described by two people of such opposing temperaments and points of view. Wakefield is all animation and colour and youthful prejudice; his book moves with the swiftness of those eager expeditions through the colony. Dieffenbach is sober, judicial in his views and statements, rather heavy-handed in narrative, and possessed of that stability of character which Jerningham so entirely lacked. The difference is well seen in their descriptions of the Cook Strait whalers. Wakefield is the man of sensibility, jotting down his impressions as they crowd upon him—the appearance of the cottages, the laughter of the whalers' half-caste children, the dignified mien of Dicky Barrett's wife, the men at work, calling to his mind Retzsch's grim illustrations to a ballad of Schiller, and less poetical, the 'intolerable' stench of the carcasses on the beach.[5] Dieffenbach also mentions the stench, but passes it off with 'this was disregarded, so great was the interest I felt in the whole process'. He describes the process, adds comments on the morals and racial characteristics of the community, then craves permission to give a short account of 'that interesting and valuable animal—the whale', which he does in exact scientific terms.[6] The one passage is the work of a reporter of genius, the other of a man who was primarily a scientist.

But Dieffenbach was a scientist at a time before science was split into a number of narrow specialisms, and besides recording the natural wonders seen during his travels, he wrote at length and with great understanding of the Maoris, with whom he almost invariably established the most friendly relations. Not being embroiled, as Wakefield was, in dubious commercial transactions, he could meet them on common ground, and in one passage he deprecates the 'arrogant and ridiculous prejudices which are too frequently characteristic of a European traveller'. He himself was remarkably free from prejudice. Of a tribe met near Tongariro he says, 'they . . . appeared to be in a very primitive state, which, however, was not, in my opinion, at all to their disadvantage.' Again, in discussing the extermination of native races by the 'civilized' Europeans, he remarks pertinently, 'the lion that tears the deer into pieces is not therefore made of nobler material.' And elsewhere he is quite explicit: 'I am of opinion that man, in his desires, passions, and intellectual faculties, is the same, whatever be the colour of his skin. . . .'[7]

Travels in New Zealand cannot be called a lively book, nor was literary grace a part of Dieffenbach's equipment. This, for example, is culled from his description of the silica terraces at Rotorua: 'The concretions assume interesting forms of mamillary stalagmites of the colour of milk-white chalcedony. . . .' To go to Dieffenbach for rhapsodies is useless, but the polysyllables are themselves signs of an undeviating strength of purpose and of a seriousness that he brought to bear on some of the fundamental issues of colonization. While not aligning himself with any of the warring factions, missionary, Company, or Government—he was, in fact, highly critical of each—as a theorist but even more as a man, he sympathized with a native people whose extinction then seemed almost inevitable. He found no comfort in a complacent doctrine of the survival of the fittest, and in an exceedingly wise chapter, 'How to Legislate for the Natives of New Zealand?', he anticipated conclusions we have reached only after bitter and costly experience. Equally percipient in his own field of the natural sciences, he seems to have been unique in foreseeing the results of bringing alien plants and animals into the colony. 'What a chain of alterations,' he exclaims, '. . . takes place from the introduction by man of a single animal into a country where it was before unknown!' Such wisdom is rare among colonists who, if they do not, as Dieffenbach too sweepingly says, devote themselves 'solely to the acquisition of money', are, from necessity and ignorance as much as from greed, careless of nature's interests and remote posterity's.[8] It was a misfortune for New Zealand that Dieffenbach did not himself remain as a colonist; after two years he returned to Europe, and his warnings and advice, locked away in two formidable volumes, went unheeded.

Among the descriptive books published in some profusion during the early years of settlement, these two contrasting and complementary works are pre-eminent. Other colonists and temporary sojourners touch on localities unvisited by Wakefield and Dieffenbach, or carry the chronological record farther, or bring their quotas to the score of controversy; but in essentials they add little to the ample accounts given by those writers. Of lesser works, only *Savage Life and Scenes* (1847) by George French Angas introduces any marked novelty into the somewhat stereotyped pattern of *Travels*, *Rambles*, *Narratives*, and *Adventures*. A young man of ample means and artistic inclinations, Angas left England on an antipodean grand tour which took him first to South Australia. There, he casually relates, 'one evening . . . I took it into my head to visit New Zealand'. A friend, he explains, had shown him some beautifully ornamented Maori weapons, and, attracted by their workmanship, he went to bed that evening to dream of 'native "pahs", and stately tattooed chiefs'. The next morning the youthful artist was on board a schooner bound for the European settlements of New Zealand.[9]

The *pas* and the stately chiefs, Angas discovered on arrival, were indeed fast becoming the substance of dreams, and moved by the melancholy picture of decay, he resolved 'to preserve memorials of the skill and ingenuity of a race of savages, who themselves ere long may pass away, and become, like their houses, matters of history. . . .' It was thus very much in the spirit of the antiquarian that he moved about the country, carefully recording with pencil and brush tombs, storehouses, implements, canoes, and a multitude of the still-surviving 'stately chiefs' with their wives, children, and slaves. In search of mementoes, human and material, he made arduous journeys into remote parts of the North Island, meeting always with the utmost friendliness from the natives. 'My mission amongst them,' he explains, 'was one of peace: I did not covet their land; and my coming from Europe for the purpose of representing their chiefs and their country was considered by them as a compliment.' Endowed with all of Dieffenbach's tolerance but with none of his solemnity (his temperamental affinities were rather with Earle), he entered fully into Maori life, noting and enjoying the hospitality of the people, their natural gaiety, their delight in repartee and wit. Transient observer though he was, Angas acquired an insight into the native mind denied to many a seasoned colonist. With prophetic accuracy he wrote, 'The Maori has now his eyes open: he looks forward; and in the perspective of a dark and gloomy future, he sees his children's land no longer their own, and his proud and swarthy race disappearing before the encroaching European. He broods over this; for he loves his country and the rights of his ancestors, and he will fight for his children's land.'[10]

With tragic irony, in the years preceding the conflict which Angas foretold, as the result of specialized studies by officials and missionaries, it became possible for the first time to form a balanced appreciation of the Maoris and their culture. In 1854 Edward Shortland published the first edition of his unfortunately titled *Traditions and Superstitions of the New Zealanders*, a work that continued the scientific investigation of the Maoris begun by the navigators, as it anticipated the methods and many of the conclusions of modern anthropology. This book and the slighter *Maori Religion and Mythology* (1882) are rich evidence of a highly cultivated mind which ranged easily and soberly over the whole field of Maori life, analysing, recording, describing, but rarely condemning in the lofty manner of so many nineteenth-century writers. As far as possible, he attempted to meet the natives on their own ground and to place the details he recorded in their living context. 'I particularly instructed my informant,' he writes, 'to tell his tale as if he were relating it to his own people, and to use the same words that he would use if he were recounting similar tales to them when assembled in a sacred house.'[11] As intelligent as he was sympathetic, his keenly analytical mind probed the confusion on which so much prejudice is based. 'The term savage . . . is very indefinite in actual signification,' he remarks and goes on to point out that there is 'as great a distinction between the highest and lowest states of savage condition, as between the highest and lowest states of civilization.'[12] Shortland's contemporary, the missionary Richard Taylor, was rather more prone to condemn and, further, to indulge in theorizings which would attribute to the Maoris an origin in the lost tribes of Israel. But moralizings and fanciful speculations apart, his *Te Ika a Maui* (1855) revealed an interest in mythology rare among missionaries (native traditions, Shortland noted, were usually dismissed by them as emanating from 'the great enemy of mankind') as well as a genuine understanding of many native institutions.[13] For example, his definition of *tapu* as 'a religious observance, established for political purposes' could scarcely be bettered, and he showed a truer appreciation of its function than did Shortland.[14]

The work of such men would, one might imagine, have swept away for ever crude misconceptions about the Maoris, and throughout the eighteen-fifties their testimony was powerfully reinforced by the superb collections which Sir George Grey issued to the world. The people who had conceived and perpetuated the contents of the *Mythology and Traditions of the New Zealanders* (1854) were clearly neither rude barbarians nor, on the other hand, guileless children of nature. The account of the primal parents, Rangi and Papa, the revolt of their children, and the final triumph of their last-born, Tu-matuenga, fierce man, formed a myth of creation lacking neither in sublimity nor in logic—though the logic, it is true, was that of a non-scientific age and a non-European system of thought. Then came the myths of the demigods, Tawhaki, Rupe, Tinirau, Rata, but supreme amongst them Maui, personification of all the admired qualities of a race, a hero whose end, part tragic part farcical, part obscene, symbolized the story of man's eternal war with death and man's eternal defeat: 'And we have this proverb, "Men make heirs, but death carries them off." ' Next were the traditions that kept alive the memory of an ancient homeland and the circumstances of the migration to Aotearoa. Here the Maori historian was not afraid to mingle the elements of mundane farce and high epic in something like their due proportions. It was no Helen who launched the fleet on its journey to Aotearoa but Toi', burdened with the fruits of crime, a pet dog heedlessly devoured: 'the dog howled in the belly of Toi', "Ow!" ... Then Toi' held his mouth as close as ever he could, but the dog still kept on howling in his inside.' Thus from trivial causes sprang war and strife until a returning voyager told of the 'beauty of this country of Aotea', and some of the war-weary determined to migrate, bearing with them the noble words of a sage, 'Now do you, my dear children, depart in peace, and when you reach the place you are going to, do not follow after the deeds of Tu', the god of war . . . but rather follow quiet and useful occupations. . . . Depart, and dwell in peace with all, leave war and strife behind you here. Depart, and dwell in peace.' The canoe voyages, as befitted their importance, were commemorated in a cycle of legends, replete with miraculous incidents and Herculean feats, for the canoe ancestors were still of heroic mould: 'These men were giants: Tama-te-kapua was nine feet high, Rua' was eleven feet high. There have been no men since that time as tall as those heroes.' Then came the legends, half fiction, half tradition, with which the nakedness of Aotearoa itself had been clothed—the complicated adventures of Paoa, a kind of Maori Humphry Clinker, the romantic tale of Hinemoa and Tutanekai, the story of the rival sorcerers, Kiki of the Waikato and Tamure of Kawhia, and others equally entertaining.[15]

In this collection was gathered the coherent record of a people imaginative, not incurious about the nature of things, and above all endowed with a profound feeling for their own past. It should have gained for them interest and respect, but on his own showing its significance was lost even on Grey himself. In a preface to the English translation—published as *Polynesian Mythology* (1855)—he elaborately explains that he gathered the traditions to aid him in his official dealings with the Maoris, and from the 'same sense of duty' published them for the benefit of others 'whose duty it may be hereafter to deal with the natives. . . .' The mingling of the sublime, the miraculous, and the mundane was evidently not to his taste, for, though comparing Polynesian mythology favourably with that of the Saxons, the Celts, and the Scandinavians, he characterized the collection as 'puerile'. He was prepared to admit, however, that 'the native races, who believed in these traditions or superstitions, are in no way deficient in intellect. . . .'[16]

Scholarship has had many unconscious benefactors, and we need not reproach Grey for his prejudices since they do not seem to have led to any serious distortion of his material. As far as one with no first-hand knowledge of the Maori language can judge, his translations are reasonably close to the originals; the diction is fairly simple, the construction and idiom are Maori rather than English (for this Grey offers a half apology), while for two of his collections—the *Traditions* and the *Proverbial and Popular Sayings of the Ancestors of the New Zealand Race* (1857)—he anticipated the wishes of future students by publishing both originals and translations; the third, the *Poems, Traditions, and Chaunts of the Maories* (1853), he published only in Maori, wisely perhaps, since the qualities of Maori poetry are such as to defy translation: the splendid hyperboles tend to emerge in English as mere bombast; the natural imagery, which came inevitably to the Maori mind, is uncomfortably reminiscent of a later school of New Zealand poetry; and an elaborate apparatus of footnotes and verbal explanations is not much help in understanding, mentally and emotionally, the many local and mythological references. Even in the time of Shortland and Grey the subtler kinds of native poetry were little more than relics for the archaeologist.

The story of the Maori people had now been placed on record, and as the colony's first two crowded decades drew to their close, New Zealand was to rise to the dignity of a full-length history in two volumes based on sources that included 'ninety volumes, two hundred pamphlets, and nearly a hundredweight of parliamentary papers'. The hero of this feat of documentary digestion was a military surgeon, Arthur S. Thomson, who spent eleven years in the country attached to the 58th Regiment and on his return to England published *The Story of New Zealand: Past and Present—Savage and Civilized* (1859). Equipped as he was with the urbanity of a Dumont d'Urville, the scientific thoroughness of a Shortland, the liveliness of a Wakefield, and unparalleled industry, no man could have been better qualified than Thomson to survey the accumulation of writings on New Zealand and to weave the scattered strands into a connected whole. The *Story* is comprehensive in scope, progressing by logical stages from a description of the natural environment and native customs and history to a full account of European discovery and settlement. Based though it is on a multitude of sources, it is no formless compilation; every section bears upon it the impress of an independent mind, even the chapter on natural history, which is elivened by references to the 'sentimental settlers' who 'designate New Zealand the Britain of the southern hemisphere' and by sensitive descriptions of the native forest. In the history of the post-Waitangi years, besides steering a way through the complex events of politics, native affairs, and government, Thomson found space to record fascinating trifles of social history. Each settlement, he notes, acquired its distinguishing epithet: 'thus there was an Auckland cove, a Wellington swell, a Nelson snob, a Taranaki exquisite, an Otago cockney, and a Canterbury pilgrim'. Acutely aware of marked colonial tendencies, he observed that children grew up 'smart in the way of making money, but in a wild state of intellectual degradation', and in a more familiar passage affirmed, 'Ditchers are more esteemed than poets, and those sciences alone are thought worth attention which confer immediate benefit.' But critical as he was of the present, Thomson could not deny himself the Pisgah sight which was already becoming established as a convention of New Zealand writing; in the ultimate union of the Maoris with the European settlers, he saw the realization of Gibbon's 'once visionary hope', that 'the Hume of the Southern Hemisphere' would 'spring from among the cannibal races of New Zealand.'[17]

Thus New Zealand's first historian, invoking the names of

European literature and addressing an audience beyond the confines of 'England's most distant colony'—the phrase is his.[18] Indeed, not only the manner but also the direction of the invocation was habitual with the writers of that time. Those who produced books did so not for the benefit of their fellow-colonists but for a public at 'Home'—whether officials of the Colonial Office, or common readers in search of information spiced with adventure, or scholars, or the vague but desirable class of 'intending emigrants'. But besides these books, published in England for an English audience, there was a literature (more accurately a mass of printed matter) which, if not indigenous, was intended for consumption in the colony itself. There were the newspapers, ground forth in the colony's earliest days—in its pre-natal days, in fact, and on one occasion with the aid of a mangle—the newspapers, with their violent political quarrels and their rich invective. Then, founded in homesick emulation of the *Edinburgh* and *Blackwood's*, were the short-lived quarterlies and magazines, which debated with high seriousness the issues of the day. Last, there was colonial verse, finding a home in advertising sheets, in meagre pamphlets, even on occasion in official gazettes. This rank exotic, imprinted nevertheless with thoughts and feelings found nowhere else, is worth a more than casual glance.

For, in spite of Thomson's epigram—'Ditchers are more esteemed than poets'—the art of versification was by no means neglected in early colonial New Zealand. On the contrary, the antipodean soil was to prove as congenial to the Victorian habit of poeticizing as to those imported weeds which alarmed the settlers by their monstrous growth. Many of the newspapers made a regular and prominent feature of their 'Poets' Corner', while some employed or patronized an official versifier who turned out topical verses on suitable occasions and in the intervals supplied the colonial demand for sentiment on such themes as 'The Sister's Grave', 'The Missionary Infant's Tomb', 'He Never Smiled Again', 'The Rose in the Burial Ground', 'To Clarinda', 'Bonnie May', and so forth.

The more official kinds of verse were generally concerned with social activities—anniversary celebrations, funerals, ceremonies at the opening of public buildings, and the less solemn gatherings that went under the generic name of 'social'. At a social a poet-entertainer would often sing his original verses, calling on the audience to join in the chorus, in the manner of the popular comedian of a past epoch. Hocken remarks of the acknowledged laureate of the Otago settlement, 'Barr was a general favourite.... At a gathering he was pretty sure to come down and sing one or two of his new compositions for the good of the company.'[19] A rather similar figure in Canterbury was C. J. Martin, whose verses were collected under the title of *Martin's Locals* (1862). These 'locals', as their name suggests, were rough verses improvised for a special occasion, exploiting the resources of colonial slang and introducing more or less recondite allusions to local celebrities and events. At their best they show a facility in rhyming and a zest in the manipulation of words that are evidence of some intellectual alertness. But they were written for the moment and essentially for a local audience; they are now somewhat pointless; the colonial idiom ('new-chum', 'shicer', 'top-sawyer') has been long superseded; they are survivals from an age rougher but more vigorous than our own.[20]

Despite their limitations, the 'locals' expressed and fostered what may be grandiloquently termed the 'sense of the community'—a feeling of cohesion among individuals, a consciousness of common origins and aims. Something similar is true of verses written in the difficult years that immediately followed settlement, the verse of disillusion. The positive note of disillusion, however, is rarely sounded. It may be found in lines by the vivacious 'Sarah, the first wife of the Rev. John Raven':

> *We left our homes with hearts elate,*
>   *Utopian visions dreaming;*
> *'Adieu,' we cried, 'to tax and rate,*
> *Adieu to wrangling and debate,*
> *Adieu to strife 'twixt Church and State,*
>   *And welcome hope and freedom!'*
>   . . . .
> *Alas! alack! the space how far*
>   *'Twixt things that seem and things that are....*[21]

It is heard, with a sourer inflection, from another Canterbury pilgrim, Dr. Rouse:

> *But I have located here;*
> *No alternative, I fear,*
> *But to make the best of thee,*
> *Only longing to be free.* . . .[22]

But this was the work of the sophisticated. Such sentiments would have been regarded by the simpler and more typical versifier as highly treasonable. It was his mission, he considered, not to dwell on the discomforts and disappointments of life in the colony (they were sufficiently obvious), but to gloss them over or to point out their compensations. This he did in a variety of ways. Elaborating a favourite theme of the colonial rhetorician, he urged the colonists, potential as well as actual, to consider their privilege as founders of a nation:

> *Come, be a nation's honored sires,*
> *The subject of all future lyres.* . . .[23]

Or he dwelt on future rewards, either for the settlers themselves or their children:

> *While, through all the future gleaming,*
> *A bright golden promise runs,*
> *And its happy light is streaming*
> *Of the greatness of our sons.*[24]

Again, he painted a rosy picture of the colony, often contrasting its freedom and prosperity with the comparative wretchedness of Britain. The natural sequel was an invitation to migrate:

> *Then ye who rule with sov'reign sway,*
>   *Around our fathers' shore,*
> *Leave not the gaunt and houseless wretch,*
>   *To perish at your door!*
> *O send him HERE, and he will soon*
>   *Be housed, and clothed, and fed.* . . .[25]

Sometimes the versifier put on the mantle of preacher and issued exhortations to effort in familiar nineteenth-century terms. The *Wellington Independent* thus urged its readers:

> *'Tis action, Work, which nerves the soul,*
> *'Tis strife which gives it strength to bear*
> *Then up and onward to the goal....*[26]

And thus the *Lyttelton Times*:

> *And this career pursue;*
> *On earth increase and multiply,*
> *Replenish and subdue!*[27]

Though so clearly devoid of the slightest literary merit, such poeticizings have some historical and representative interest. These, it is perhaps fair to assume, were among the reflections of the ordinary settler, the man who was induced to migrate by the propaganda of the New Zealand Company, who travelled steerage to the colony, who finally established himself on his own section of land. By such ponderings he consoled himself in those difficult years for the non-fulfilment of hopes and promises. This was the rough philosophy that nerved him to persevere with work that was so often monotonous and ill-rewarded. If he himself were not to 'reap the benefits', at least his children would; for moral accountancy demanded some credit entry to counterbalance the visible debit. His lot might be hard, but think of the destitute millions in the old world! And though now obscure, in the future—perhaps a century or so hence—his name and his achievement would be recognized by a grateful posterity.

It is a conviction that is embedded, like much of the stock-in-trade of the Poets' Corner, in the work of the most prolific early versifier, William Golder, a Scottish settler in the Hutt valley. A poetaster of large ambitions and unequalled verbosity, for twenty years he issued to the settlers and gentry of Port Nicholson a series of verse collections and narrative poems, epic in their scope and proportions, which ranged from *The New Zealand Minstrelsy* (1851) ('a tribute to the early settlers of our Colony') to *The Philosophy of Love* (1871). Of his successive pamphlets, with their faint type, their elaborately worded title-pages, and their amateurish format, only one, *The Pigeons' Parliament* (1854), is today other than a collector's curiosity. Intended as a satire in the traditional manner, *The Pigeons' Parliament* gives a pungent record of colonial life as it appeared to a labouring immigrant with that itch for self-improvement not uncommon in his class and his time. We note the rough and often shrewdly drawn portraits of prominent colonists, such as this of Edward Gibbon Wakefield:

> *So there was one*
> *Some would declare the moon upon*
> *His pate had struck;—while some would shew,*
> *More than the others wished to know,*
> *That in him sound philanthropy,*
> *With all considerate charity,*
> *Was parent of each thought or deed.*

The details of some obscure incident dramatically spring to life, as in these exhilarating lines describing a threat of native invasion:

> *And sweating sawyers leave the saw,*
> *And shoulder arms to enforce the law:*
> *Hoping the job might never cease—*
> *'Long live the wars! a fig for peace!'—*
> *So long's no skirmish happens here*
> *But fing'ring pay and keeping cheer.*[28]

But extracts, since they draw attention to obvious imperfections of detail, do less than justice to this rough ballad. It is, indeed, in the real sense a popular ballad with all the qualities of its kind—vigour, broad humour, crudeness of versification and expression, topical and local appeal, and, by virtue of its spontaneity, a total effect that obscures the glaring defects of its parts. (And Golder carried on the ballad-monger's tradition by canvassing personally for subscribers, hawking his works about for sale, and in the case of a later book, printing it himself.) This doggerel epic has, above all, a vitality that one expects and so rarely finds in the literature of a 'new country' (outworn and misleading phrase), a vitality that is expressed in occasional rhythms, in the ideas original to the point of absurdity, in the lively words and images that Golder's fancy throws upon the page.

To contrast with the formless exuberance of Golder's work, there are the neat verses of John Barr of Craigielea, collected in his *Poems and Songs, Descriptive and Satirical* which was published in Edinburgh in 1861 with the help of a group of patrons. Barr, too, was a Scot, but more wisely than the bard of Port Nicholson he seldom ventured beyond the limits prescribed by his own vernacular and its verse tradition. This was his main source of strength, and it was an advantage that the Otago settlement in its earlier years sufficiently resembled a Scottish community for a genuine continuance of the vernacular tradition to be possible; it was small, comparatively shut off from the rest of New Zealand, and dominated by Scottish settlers whose patriotic and religious fervour had become the more intense through exile. A microcosm of Scottish society, the settlement clung tenaciously to its native customs and speech which were, nevertheless, changing under the pressure of New Zealand conditions. The contrast between the traditional ways on one hand and the abhorrent colonial tendencies on the other gave ample scope for a social satirist, and it was as such that Barr excelled.

A recurrent object of his criticism is the colonial preoccupation with money and material things to the detriment of the soul and the mind. And, true to a common vernacular convention, the embodiment of a particular vice is very often a woman. One such passage, the close of a piece of invective aimed at an avaricious shrew, also illustrates a frequent device of his verse, the expansion of an English expression by a more vivid and concrete phrase in dialect:

> There are some folks get wealth, and it brings them a curse,
> For they worship a God that's wrapped up in a purse:
> You're a perfect skinflint, and a puir scart-the-bowl;
> O woman! be wise, and think mair of your soul.

Often he makes his effect by means of simple irony, as when a Scottish Polonia advises her son on the choice of a wife:

> *Get ane can drub through dub and mire,*
> *Wi' muckle buits and tackets;*
>
> . . . . .
>
> *And Jock, my man, when ye have weans,*
> *Ne'er fash wi' education;*
> *But pack them off to herd the kye,*
> *Or to some shepherd's station.*

His language was well adapted to describe colonial activities and had power to assimilate the common terms of the settler's vocabulary. Lines like the following have an almost muscular quality, a suggestion of tension and effort that admirably represents the movements described:

> *For either I'm mawin', or thrashin', or sawin',*
> *Or grubbin' the hills wi' the ferns covered fairly.*
> *Grub away, tug away, toil till you're weary,*
> *Haul oot the toot roots and everything near ye.*[29]

It was a modest talent that saw the light in Otago's first years. Yet it may not be altogether fanciful to see in Barr's small success the potentialities of some more considerable achievement. If the isolation of Otago had been preserved, if Barr had been not the first and last but the father of a line of vernacular poets, would a local culture have taken root in the south? The question is unanswerable, for Barr's small book might well have arrived in Otago with a shipload of prospectors attracted by the discovery of gold. Overnight the narrow, intense life of the small Scottish community was transformed, the possibility of independent growth denied. Barr founded no tradition, and when his medium was used by later poets, at its best it could be only a literary importation, mellifluous, quaint, but sterile, as in Jessie Mackay:

> *The hand is to the plough an' the e'e is to the trail:*
> *The river-boatie dances wi' her heid to the gale. . . .*[30]

Nor were the other settlements exempt from similar change. Whether from gold discoveries, or Maori wars, or some other concomitant of 'progress', during the next two decades any signs of regional or local development were decisively checked. New Englands were not founded in the mid-nineteenth century, and by the end of the next period Otago was to have produced not successors to the rustic John Barr but the ominous figure of Julius Vogel.

IV
The Period of Expansion

If a person and a turning-point were needed to mark a new phase in New Zealand history, they might be found in Samuel Butler and in January 1860, the date of his arrival in Canterbury. In outward circumstances this young settler resembled James Edward FitzGerald: both were graduates of Cambridge, both were writers and amateurs of art, and both sought in 'England's most distant colony' release from the irksome restraints of the old world. But by 1860 the era of the 'pilgrims' was ended. Men no longer came to New Zealand burdened with grandiose theories or self-dedicated to the building of ideal states. A new spirit was abroad, a spirit that is described—and also revealed—in *A first Year in Canterbury Settlement* (1863). 'New Zealand,' wrote Butler, 'seems far better adapted to develop and maintain in health the physical than the intellectual nature. The fact is, people here are busy making money; that is the inducement which led them to come in the first instance, and they show their sense by devoting their energies to the work.'[1]

The fact is, it might be added, that though so exceptional a colonist, Butler was in some respects a representative of the new men who were to rise to wealth and influence in the next few decades. With its account of the systematic search for unoccupied lands, its shrewd calculation of ways and means, its intensive preoccupation with profit and investment, *A First Year* shows clearly enough that Butler was not uncomfortably at odds with this money-getting society. True, as he often testifies, the pursuit of wealth went on in a setting where the end might well be forgotten in the magnificence of the scene. 'The mountains were pale as ghosts'; 'the scenery is quite equal in grandeur to that of Switzerland'; 'I was struck almost breathless by the wonderful mountain that burst on my sight'—the letters are strewn with tributes like these, though Butler followed up the last one with the comment, 'A mountain here is only beautiful if it has good grass on it. . . . If it is good for sheep, it is beautiful, magnificent, and all the rest of it; if not, it is not worth looking at.'[2]

'Good for sheep'—that was the final criterion. Yet, ignoble as they might appear in their sublime setting, New Zealand men and New Zealand society possessed qualities that Butler in his search for emancipation could only approve—the freedom from 'much nonsense in the old country', the comparative lack of conventionalism and formality, the absence of sectarianism, and the 'healthy, sensible tone in conversation'. 'But,' he concluded, 'it does not do to speak about John Sebastian Bach's "Fugues", or pre-Raphaelite pictures.'[3]

Butler's pleasant, not uncritical picture of life in Canterbury is one which, with modifications, would have fitted the greater part of the colony between the eighteen-sixties and the nineties. During those years the North Island, bush-covered and intermittently harassed by Maori wars, lost its ascendancy to the South where, through the agency of gold and an expanding pastoral industry, settlement was pushed back from the coastal nuclei formed in the first two decades to the mountainous limits of the interior. New Zealand's centre of gravity shifted outwards; its social life, concentrated to a far smaller extent in the original settlements, now spread out amongst farms and sheep stations, gold-fields and sawmills, and for briefer intervals amongst militia posts and military camps. With this change came a corresponding change in the people themselves. The Company settlers, the 'old identity', as they were termed in affectionate derision, found themselves swamped by men of a different type, a 'new iniquity' heterogeneously composed of squatters, shearers, gold-miners, volunteers, and professional soldiers.

Campaigns are not recorded by an army on the march; the most that soldiers can be expected to contribute are materials for the historian—the plan of battle, the official despatch, the personal letter hastily scrawled between engagements. This pioneering period of New Zealand history, even in its more pacific aspects, bore some resemblance to a military campaign, and its prose

4

literature is best described as source material for an historian. The letters of a settler were gathered and printed by parents or friends; a soldier or a squatter kept a diary which in the leisure of English retirement he refurbished for publication; a vicar's wife, a governess, a school-teacher, a housewife, impelled by those strange motives which lie behind the writing of fiction, poured out her heart by candlelight and, through some freak of chance, found a publisher. These, in the main, were the circumstances in which New Zealand experience throughout a generation was set on record. Not surprisingly the results, with few exceptions, are fragmentary, unsatisfying, often boring. Where is the colour of that life, where the humour, where the tussle between man and man and the struggle with nature? So we complain as we trudge through dreary (and often inaccurate) *réchauffés* of New Zealand history, accounts of the moa, pointless anecdotes, fatuous 'adventures'. The probability is, we conclude, that the fitting transcript of those years never reached the printing-press. It may have passed with the cycles of yarns that circulated among the restless army of 'travelling labour'. It may have been dissipated in the warmth of camp-fires or in the shearers' quarters on summer evenings. It may have been locked in minds unschooled and inarticulate.

Of published literature—and the rest is speculation—the largest and perhaps the most interesting group is made up of the novels and memoirs which have as their background the farming industry, the most stable feature of that troubled landscape. The majority of such books are cut to a relatively uniform pattern, conforming to that of most settlers' lives—emigration, settlement, experiences in remote country districts, material success or failure—a formula elastic enough to include a number of distinct types and a diversity of experience. Pride of place must be given to the feminine and domestic type, and not merely on grounds of chronology, for, as Lady Barker noted, 'a lady's influence' in the colony was 'very great'. 'She represents refinement and culture ... and her footsteps on a new soil such as this should be marked by a trail of light.'[4]

It was an admonition already well heeded by New Zealand's first lady novelist, Mrs. J. E. Aylmer, in concocting *Distant Homes* or *The Graham Family in New Zealand* (1862), though here the light was subdued to the dull glow of didactic piety and domestic sentiment. Not that *Distant Homes* is lacking in incident; on the contrary, from the first day the Grahams touch the barbarous shores of the colony they are plunged into a very maelstrom of adventure. With as fine a disregard for fact as was shown by her probable exemplar, the author of *The Swiss Family Robinson*, Mrs. Aylmer exposes her characters to the perils of 'the volcano of Mount Egmont' (' "the old mountain never gives us warning in vain" ', quoth a worthy salt), and after their arrival in Canterbury, to the delicious terrors of a Maori insurrection. Before reaching this climax, however, the authoress has discoursed freely on colonial and native customs, either in her own person or through stratagems such as this:

' "But what do they worship? Do they bow down to idols? or pray to the sun, moon, and stars?"

' "You have asked me a very difficult question, Lucy, and one that will require a great deal of explanation. . . ." '

By the joint heroism of Captain Graham and his wife, the insurrection is quelled, and having absorbed a Hollywood-serial portion of incident and a handbook on New Zealand besides (all in the space of 199 pages), the reader leaves the Graham family with the fervent hope that 'peace and good-will may reign through the length and breadth of our precious colony of New Zealand'.[5]

The work of Lady Barker, set in the same locality, may also be described as domestic, but with a difference. Wisely she restricted herself to the range of colonial life that she knew, the often trivial but never uninteresting experiences of an Englishwoman (more exactly, an English gentlewoman), confronted by an entirely new order of society and by the multitudinous duties of a squatter's wife. She is best known by *Station Life in New Zealand* (1870) and *Station Amusements in New Zealand* (1873), books which more than any others of the period are exempt from the charges of dullness and banality. Together they give the most complete and satisfying picture of that ample life on the plains and foot-hills of Canterbury before the squattocracy had hardened into a caste and the tending of sheep into a highly organized industry. The innocent pleasures are there, and the calamities, such as the loss of a child or that overwhelming disaster, the great snow-storm of 1867. The domestic worries, usually centred in the servants' quarters, are described with feminine particularity and those pastoral activities which did not offend a lady's delicacy and nineteenth-century proprieties. The weather, inevitably in the conditions of that life, becomes a major character whose moods and whims from week to week are minutely recorded; while the settings are sketched with the limpid spontaneity of a writer who rarely, if ever, perpetrates a *cliché*. It is, of course, the pastoral scene surveyed from the topmost social pinnacle; but Lady Barker's viewpoint is aristocratic rather than snobbish, and though aware of the gulf between a lady and the wife of a 'cockatoo', she had learned enough from colonial experience to write in her second book of 'the class whom we foolishly speak of as the lower orders'.[6]

Into these two books she packed the chief impressions of some five years spent in New Zealand; the residue, with careful husbandry, she converted into sketches, semi-fictional in form, which are scattered through a number of collections. Written ostensibly for children and concealed by such titles as *Stories About* (1871), *A Christmas Cake* (1871), and *Boys* (1875), they are nevertheless surprisingly mature in theme and treatment. 'Christmas Day in New Zealand,' one of the four quarters of the *Christmas Cake*, is indeed the best recorded example of a shepherd's yarn. In transposition some crudities of speech and incident have doubtless been ironed out, but enough remains to evoke the rich, smoke-filled atmosphere of the shepherds' concourse assembled for the purpose of 'capping yarns'. Some enterprising publisher will one day reissue these sketches to give them the modest fame they deserve.

A third and contrasting version of the domestic formula is to be found in two novels published in 1874, *A Strange Friendship* and *Over the Hills and Far Away*, by Mrs. C. Evans. The writer's ambitions and the prevailing tone of these pathetic books can best be illustrated from the preface of *Over the Hills*: 'Thinking of the mighty waste of waters which separates me from the home-country, I feel tempted to exclaim, "Oh, mighty ocean which divides us, hush your roar awhile! Oh, wild winds, cease to moan! and let them hear my voice in England!" ' They are the wish-fulfilments of an exiled gentlewoman, and their mood is one of pensive nostalgia. Mrs. Evans's families (all gentlefolk and clearly the colonial progeny of Charlotte Brontë's Lucys and Rochesters) are conveyed to New Zealand where, with few pioneering preliminaries, they establish themselves in country-houses. There they exchange books and periodicals—the heroes their *Cornhills* and *Edinburghs*, the heroines *Middlemarch*, *Idylls of the King*, *Lady Adelaide's Oath*—speculate about the social position and origin of their neighbours (' "I wonder who the Ainsleighs are, and what part of England they come from." '), discuss 'friends at home' and 'the people and the places where we had grown up together', and indulge in elegant pastimes that have little resemblance to the simple picnics and concerts the author professes to describe. Driven by the demands of fantastic plots (which owe less to *Middlemarch* than to *Lady Adelaide's Oath*), the heroines are weighed down by domestic secrets, suffer agonies of frustration through self-imposed vows of silence, to find relief in the interminable writing up of diaries: 'He had kissed my riding-glove, and when I was safely shut in my own room, I took that glove off and hid it away in a box with a rose. . . .'[7]

There are occasional tributes to the scenery of New Zealand, but the colonial background is usually left vague where it does not intrude as something alien or even malign. When a colonial is introduced, it is as a bucolic foil to the god-like principal characters, though one minor figure is described with approval as 'one of the upper class of New Zealand working men'. Dolly, the heroine of *A Strange Friendship*, adheres with an unbending rectitude to the conventions of the Sussex 'grange' from which she has been transferred to the colony. Her sister Violet, a character of weaker moral fibre, is unable to withstand the demoralizing influence of the new environment and goes off to visit the 'fast' Madelaine Ainsleigh ('the only other girl in our own rank of life'), exclaiming defiantly to her sister-in-law, ' "I warn you, Kate . . . that I do not intend to take up any absurd prejudices. In this country, as Harry observed the other day, it is far better to be neighbourly...." ' Inevitably she comes to a bad end. The incorruptible Dolly, on the other hand, marries a titled husband who confers on her the supreme felicity of repatriation to the 'home-country', where she reigns as mistress of Curtis Knowle, his ancestral home. So was virtue rewarded and the dream of a homesick gentlewoman realized.[8]

The masculine novel, a class that shades imperceptibly into the pioneer memoir, is an even more artless narrative, tracing a single colonist's life and adventures which are often eked out by the customary accounts of New Zealand's history, flora, fauna, and 'future prospects'. A writer will announce his intention of giving 'the general reader some knowledge of New Zealand, of its short history, of its last war, and of the character of that most interesting race the Maori, in the popular form of a novel'.[9] And, in his casual way, he picks up the threads of the narrative with 'I may as well state here', or 'At this point it is necessary to overhaul a bit'.[10] Superimposed on the socially determined plot of emigration and settlement, there is in the more ambitious examples the mechanical plot of nineteenth-century fiction—an affair of crime, of mystery uncovered in a final chapter, of preposterous coincidence.

W. M. B., a representative author of this school, has retired to his native York. 'In the course of an eventful and active life, during a long residence at the Antipodes,' he explains in 'My Preface', 'it had often been my lot or necessity to turn my hand to very many occupations and callings... and since my return to England, finding myself with "nothing to do," I determined to add that of an author to the number.' The result, published in 1874 as *The Narrative of Edward Crewe or Life in New Zealand*, is a thinly disguised autobiography in which the author strings together his experiences as a colonist, inserting many curious observations on the antipodes and life in general. After a boyhood in York and an education at Rugby ('At the latter seat of learning we acquired—first, truthfulness, ever scorning to tell a lie; secondly, the ways of a gentleman; and lastly, a skilful acquaintance with the noble games of cricket and football.'), he decides to emigrate, admitting with candour his disinclination and mental incapacity for any of the professions. He lands at Auckland, is by turns trader, bush-whacker, sawmiller, land-speculator until finally he strikes it rich as a gold-miner and returns with his wealth to England. Into the shapeless receptacle provided by this narrative, the writer stuffs all manner of oddments whose nature and variety can be gauged by a few page-headings: Drunken Bay, Buying a Wife, Venomous Spider—Katipo, Pig Hunting, 'Always a Gentleman', St. Thomas Aquinas (described as 'the greatest intellectual swell in the Church some 600 years ago . . . a man of the right sort'), No Sunday in the Bush, How to Rub Fire. The book is as raw and ill-assorted as this inventory; with its gusto, its profusion of crude ideas and cruder anecdotes, its loose colloquialisms, it suggests the yarning assemblage of the shearing-shed or miners' camp, and from that fact derives its virtue. It is a document, both to entertain and to instruct, transcribing faithfully and uncritically the surface agitation of the unformed society to which the author himself had temporarily belonged.[11]

There is a notable difference in Scottish versions of the emigrant-pioneer novel, exemplified by Alexander Bathgate's *Waitaruna* (1881) and by the two novels of Dugald Ferguson, *Bush Life* (1893) and *Mates* (1911), which, though falling outside the strict chronological limits of the period, belongs spiritually to the same epoch. In these books, set principally in Otago, the pioneer hero's life is unfolded against the same background, but its disorders and excesses are condemned both openly in the author's running commentary and by implication in the fate he metes out to his characters. Thus Gilbert Langton, the industrious cadet of *Waitaruna*, rises to the position of station-manager, while his foil, Arthur Leslie, succumbs to colonial influences, marries a barmaid, and is left drinking himself to death as the landlord of an unsavoury public house in the diggings. In Dugald Ferguson's work the same retributive justice falls on those who, through frailty or wilfulness, diverge from the strait Presbyterian path. It is no coincidence that these books enjoyed a modest local popularity at a time when the life they portrayed was receding romantically into the past, while their standards of conduct were the accepted ones among the rural *bourgeoisie* of the post-pioneer years.

Ferguson's work also illustrates, in a marked form, stylistic features common to the novels. In spite of his out-of-door man's disregard of construction and the niceties of form and expression, he rises to a certain inflated elaborateness when a situation is considered important and hence in need of some more dignified attire than the ordinary plain narrative. So, in *Bush Life*, he disposes of a character in this strain: 'Thus died Randal Howden in his thirty-fifth year, a man endowed with great natural abilities and a fierce energy, that, turned to a right end, might have won for him a glorious name in military annals. Yet, a victim to his own passions, and misled by his unconquerable egotism, and the atheistical principles that loosened his mind from a sense of all moral responsibility for his actions, these talents but enabled him to sustain for a while the part of hero of an inglorious career, whose dark record. . . .' Similarly conversation alternates between the vigorous idiom of colonial speech: ' ". . . she carefully mentioned all the young ladies that had got spliced . . . and all the others who had their chaps prospectively hooked. . . . All the married dames who had lately got kids . . . and all the old dames who had kicked, or were likely to kick the bucket . . . ." ' and melodramatic bombast in the emotional scenes: ' "What have you to complain of then?" [The villain asks of the girl he has betrayed.] "Of nothing, if I only had the mind of the brute that perishes; of nothing, if I had not been reared in affluence and love; of nothing, if my mind had not been expanded by education to enable me more fully to appreciate the advantages I have for ever forfeited; of nothing. . . ." '[12]

A feature corresponding to the widely diffused emigrant-pioneer plot and, like it, the product of similar history and social conditions is the set of 'stock characters', a few figures who appear throughout the novels with a remarkable uniformity. First there is the newly arrived immigrant, the 'new chum', whose 'verdancy' (to cite a recurrent example of pioneer wit) is the butt of the seasoned colonial. 'To be a new chum,' remarks Edward Crewe, 'is not agreeable . . . people speak to you in a pitying and patronizing manner, smiling at your real or inferred simplicity in colonial life, and altogether "sitting upon you" with much frequency and persistence.'[13] More useful for the novelist's purpose (since most people in the first few decades had been new chums) was the 'remittance man'. Some writers use him for farcical or satirical purposes, contrasting his English accent and genteel manners (the façade of moral and physical weakness) with the solid virtues of the hard-working colonial. Usually, however, he is a more formidable character, villainous or heroic, in whom a writer found it convenient to centre the mystery of the novel. He arrives in the colony under a cloud, meets there, by a miraculous series of coincidences, old friends or enemies, and ultimately clears himself of some unfounded charge; or, alternatively, he involves himself more deeply in crime, to pay the inevitable penalty in the final chapter. The minor stock figures are similarly localized characters of lesser Victorian fiction and melodrama: farcical Irishmen, dark-haired sirens, and two products more distinctive of the colonial soil—the incompetent and independent servant, who is the focus of male attention, and the misanthropic recluse, the 'hatter' in mining argot. Among such creatures of cardboard there is sometimes inserted a character of more vital interest, some person created from immediate observation. While this figure holds the stage, the writer forgets his story, genuine humour seeps in, and themes of local interest are introduced. For example, in the formless bulk of Clara Cheeseman's *A Rolling Stone* (1886), a minor character, Langridge, disentangles himself from the plot to take on local form and colour: 'there were his children; he was ambitious for them, not for himself. If it were somewhat too late in his day for the cultivation of the habits and manners of polite society, and decidedly too late for an amendment of his education, there was yet time to make his son the equal of those whom the farmer had always reverently considered as beings of a nature superior to his own, and whom he usually spoke of as the "upper classes." '[14]

These, however, are tiny and infrequent oases in a desert of facts, anecdotes, pointless descriptions, absurd melodramatic contortions. With the exception of Lady Barker's sketches, only one imaginative work handles the rural life of this period with any approach to insight. Published in 1891, *Philosopher Dick* by George Chamier does in fact express an era, as it sums up the whole class of pioneer fiction and memoirs. But it is no neglected masterpiece. In its main outlines and in many of its details it resembles most other pioneer novels: it has as its central character the conventional English migrant; it traverses the usual range of rough experience and contains the usual assortment of stock characters; it is even more amateurishly contrived than many of its kind, being lamely pieced together by diaries, letters, and long interpolated confessions in the manner of Smollett; its prose is loose and formless, cluttered with *clichés* and redundancies. What distinguishes it from the rest is the writer's critical and occasionally sardonic point of view, his ampler scale of treatment, and his approach to serious themes barely recognized by his predecessors.

Richard Raleigh, the 'philosopher' of the title (and, one may infer, a partly autobiographic creation) is a FitzGerald of fiction, a young idealist who has migrated from the old world—'a world made up of trivialities, bustle, greed, sensuality, and emptiness'—hoping to find in a new country the conditions for a life of freedom and contemplation.[15] Equipped with a library, a flute, and painting materials (for he shared the interests of the young Samuel Butler), he arrives at the men's quarters of Marino station. Here diverse types and nationalities are gathered together to lead a life which, despite its vigour and rough friendliness, is to the civilized mind scarcely above the level of brute existence. Failing to discover in these surroundings the tranquillity and freedom he seeks, Raleigh withdraws still farther into a shepherd's hut on the boundaries of the station.

The sequel, described with a clinical profusion of detail, is of remarkable interest and has a wide application, for if potential Samuel Butlers were rare among the settlers of New Zealand, conditions of isolation with their disintegrating effects on the mind were sufficiently common. For a time Raleigh exults in his solitude and independence of the world of affairs, finding fulfilment in 'communing with nature' and in art. But this mood soon yields to one of melancholy—he has learned the bitter lesson of personal insufficiency: 'In vain would he strive to rouse himself from this miserable dejection; seek for relaxation in his books, call in aid all his philosophy, or fly to his beloved palette.' And as these sources of strength and assurance fail him, he loses touch with his former associations: 'The outside world had lost all interest for him—it had almost ceased to exist to his distempered mind. . . .' He concludes that he has abandoned civilization, now endowed with all the attractions of the remote and the unattainable, 'To make a fool of myself; to bury myself in a wilderness; to seek for solitude, misery, and privation at the farthest end of the world.'[16]

The situation is convincing, though described at excessive length and with the resources of a third-rate writer when it demands those of a Dostoievsky. Raleigh is disillusioned, at odds with himself and his surroundings, a *déraciné* with all the traits of his kind. The dissipation of illusions, for example, expresses itself in a deflation of the near and the actual by contrast with what is romantic and remote. Boar-hunting, 'such as we . . . see represented in celebrated pictures by the Old Masters,' is the standard by which 'pig-sticking' is measured, with inevitable results: 'It was not a noble sport . . . nor was it conducted in a sportsmanlike manner. . . . The hunter . . . sallied forth in his ordinary costume—which was always dirty, often deficient, and never picturesque—with a couple of collies, a bull-dog, and a butcher's knife.' The 'colonial mushroom townships' are examined and found wanting in 'all the attractions of a refined civilization, the beauties of art, or the charms of old associations' —'Their existence is a ceaseless activity, their soul is *business*, and their motto "Go ahead".' And the narrator derives an ignoble satisfaction from ridiculing the sacred assumptions of his fellows. ' "Miserable fatality!" [He exalts in describing the death of the industrious station-manager.] "Lamentable perversion of the moral order of things. The good apprentice comes to an untimely end; the idle one hath long life and goodly reward." '[17]

The analysis of the hero-author's fluctuating moods provides a slender framework for the narrative and is responsible for some authentic criticism of the pioneer and for passages of telling satire. As the novel progresses, however, Raleigh relaxes his attitude of petulant detachment to become more at one with his surroundings. He expends pages on the minute details of his occupation and environment, analyses the relations between men and men and between men and animals, elaborately records the trivialities of social life and gossip: the *déraciné* has begun to send down roots.

Philosopher Dick is a baffling novel, as difficult to characterize and assess as the society it describes. The sincere is mixed with the pretentious, farce with pathos, obtuseness of thought and feeling meet one on the same page as delicacy and sympathy. In more senses than one it is a pioneer work, an attempt to impose some coherence and form upon a formless mass of experience. The attempt was undoubtedly too ambitious, it was almost certainly premature, but with little competition Chamier takes his place in the New Zealand literary hierarchy as the most distinguished novelist of its pastoral epoch.

From a distance of almost a century (and indeed to some contemporary eyes) the Maori wars of the eighteen-sixties may be seen as part of the movement which at the same time spilled men over the hinterland of Otago and Canterbury. The motives of the Europeans concerned were similar, the end—land—was the same. The difference was in the opponents: in the one island nature, in the other a native people whose suppression was effected only by a struggle as bitter on the domestic and political fronts as on the military. This confused episode in New Zealand history threw up an immense quantity of writing which is chiefly polemical in nature and, fortunately, impermanent in form. The crumbling pages of contemporary newspapers contain grim evidence of the feeling and the prejudice excited by each phase of the conflict. Even the comic journals of the time, especially those published near the scene of war, are disfigured by cartoons of a savagery which is now scarcely credible. In pamphlet literature there is a juster division of opinion between the advocates of 'the strong hand' and the 'Maoriphiles'; but a case argued in the strident and over-simplified terms of public controversy has little power of survival outside the dusty vaults of scholarship.

Hardly less impassioned are the writings of larger size and pretensions. With perhaps three or four exceptions, books on the wars and the Maoris are pamphlets writ large with none of the pamphlet's merciful brevity. Pre-eminent among the exceptions is J. E. Gorst's *The Maori King* (1864), an impartial and absorbing account written from first-hand observation by one with an intimate knowledge of the Waikato and an appreciation of Maori modes of life and thought which could then be paralleled only in Shortland. While Gorst's sympathy with the native cause is clearly and consistently expressed, he never reduces the Maori to a dehumanized symbol of injustice and suffering. 'The Maori', in fact, does not appear in Gorst, only Maoris of a diversity that might be expected from any group of human beings. There are the able and incorruptible men like Wiremu Tamihana; the waverers and schemers who clustered about the unfortunate young Maori king; the light-hearted adventurers like Wiremu Kumete who, 'having planted his crops, and having nothing else in particular to do, marched down to Taranaki,' returning from the expedition 'in time to reap his crops'; there is even the Maori bore who 'began a long speech, commencing from the creation of the world, and working slowly on towards modern times, while everybody else went to sleep'.[18] It is this perception of diversity, including humour, which makes Gorst so convincing when he is compared with equally sincere though more limited writers. The underlying causes of the wars, as he explains them, were not simple: they arose not from villainy but from confusion of aims, from lack of understanding on both sides, and among the Europeans from apathy and bewildering alternations of policy. To perceive this when the issues were so confused and the events so close was an achievement which makes Gorst one of the most remarkable men of this period. To express it in a fluent, temperate prose was an even rarer achievement which gives him a lonely eminence among those who ventured to peer beneath the events of the wars and seek their origins.

The course of the wars themselves, more especially the operations of the colonial troops, can be traced in Lieutenant T. W. Gudgeon's *Reminiscences of the War in New Zealand* (1879), modestly characterized by its author as 'a simple narrative of events, of skirmishes and expeditions grandiloquently called campaigns'. It is the work of an intelligent soldier, more concerned with the details of sieges and encounters than with the tangled motives behind them, though when he goes outside his self-imposed limits to discuss the origins of the King movement and the Hauhau religion, he is temperate and sometimes discerning. In contrast with the writings of most non-combatants, the *Reminiscences* show a refreshing absence of rancour. Gudgeon's Maori opponents are simply described as 'the enemy' or occasionally with pity as 'the poor wretches', while in giving an account of Te Kooti's escape from the Chatham islands, he ventured to doubt 'whether Europeans would have behaved with greater moderation if placed in similar circumstances'.[19] With no pretensions to 'style' and without resort to the purple patch, he succeeds in giving an adequate impression of the picturesque scene of the campaigns; and, drawing not on art but from a fund of native good sense and good feeling, he inserts touches of warmth or humour or asperity which make the book something more than a mere 'narrative of events'. Though they belonged to opposite camps, it is not unlikely that Gorst and Gudgeon could have met and discussed their points of view without heat and perhaps with agreement as to fundamentals; for, different as they were, the scholarly administrator and the campaigner shared virtues rare enough at the time—tolerance, kindliness, and clear-headedness.

They were virtues notably lacking in the writers of fiction who exploited the sensational incidents and romantic background of the wars. The first novel of this kind (if novel it can be called) was Major B. Stoney's *Taranaki: a Tale of the War* (1861) which claimed on a congested title-page to provide 'A Description of the Province previous to and during the War; also an Account (chiefly taken from the Despatches) of the Principal Contests with the Natives during that eventful Period'. This book and its successors bear some resemblance to the class of pioneer-emigrant novels, though far outclassing them in crudity of plot, in deficiency of construction, and in blatant didacticism. The typical hero is an officer newly arrived from India, the heroine the daughter of a New Zealand settler or merchant. They meet only to be parted after a brief courtship when the soldier goes off to join his regiment at the seat of war. It usually happens that he is captured by the natives, but by some stratagem escapes and, having cleared his honour, leads the heroine to the altar. A favourite conclusion is a glimpse of the two established in 'The Hall' in some part of rural England. Meanwhile the reader has again absorbed an epitome of New Zealand history and varied information about Maori customs conveyed in descriptive passages, in footnotes, or in this fashion: ' "Enough of this, kati (be quiet). I have here a decoction of the poroporo (solanum lacincatum), which will heal thy wounds." '[20] These words (a mild example of the stilted language common to the novels) are uttered by a Maori witch; for necromancy, and with it cannibalism, usually enters the books in some guise. In this particular sample, *Hine-Ra, or The Maori Scout* (1887), the dark powers are invoked to prophesy the ultimate doom of the Maori people. This again is a favourite motif, more bluntly put by the author of *Henry Ancrum* (1872), as he looks forward to the time 'when the savage Maori has disappeared—as disappear he must'.[21] Except for the winsome *wahine* inserted to supply the necessary love interest, the fictional Maori is indeed a savage, to be annihilated in mass and without compunction. In the most spectacular climax, the destruction of a party of Hauhaus is accomplished by an explosion which at the same time lays bare a reef of gold. Similar constituents, contrived with more sophistication and mingled with borrowings from Poe and Haggard, make up H. B. M. Watson's *The Web of the Spider* (1892). Worthy of greater respect, though ineffably dreary, are two reconstructions of primitive Maori life published in 1874, George H. Wilson's *Ena, or The Ancient Maori* and John White's *Te Rou; or The Maori at Home*. A good deal of scholarship is embalmed in these two novels, especially in the second, but their effect is to suggest that the Maori of pre-European times spent a necessarily short life in slaughtering and consuming his enemies, in consulting witch-doctors, and in making chaste love against an ornate scenic background.

From such turgid and tasteless compilations it is a relief to turn to the work of two men, John Logan Campbell and F. E.

Maning, who wrote of the Maoris without recourse to the spurious aids of plot and love interest. Campbell's anonymously published *Poenamo* (1881) was, he explains, in origin a family document, intended for the instruction—and, presumably, the entertainment—of his children, and given to a wider public only with reluctance. It was, he asserts, written '*currente calamo* . . . without any pretension at artistic composition'. In spite of this disarming profession, its modern sponsor, Joan Stevens, has shown that the book was laboured over for a long period before achieving its final form and, further, that it was the outcome of considerable literary contrivance—a fact that is evident from Campbell's studied manner and his liberal use of quotations and Latin or Gallic tags. Following the usual course of pioneer reminiscence, the writer describes his antecedents and youth, his migration to the 'Great Convict Land', his arrival in New Zealand (the 'sunny Great South Land' Campbell terms it), and his experiences as land-purchaser and trader in the infant settlement of Auckland.[22] The resulting narrative reveals the modest and attractive qualities of its author, it possesses a mild anecdotal charm, and occasionally at its best (as in the timber-dragging chapter) it is reminiscent of *Old New Zealand*. One wearies, however, of the all-pervading facetiousness, of the trite literary allusions, of the Caledonian sentiment. And one suspects that Campbell's attitude of affectionate condescension towards the Maoris may have been almost as formidable a barrier to understanding as the prejudices of many a less enlightened settler. In the inevitable comparison, the author of *Poenamo* must, by a large margin, yield second place to his contemporary and friend, Maning.

From the time of their publication, Maning's two books, the *History of the War in the North* (1862) and *Old New Zealand* (1863), have grown in esteem until they are now commonly regarded as 'New Zealand classics', doomed, like other classics, to be uncritically accepted more often than examined. They are, however, products of a distinct phase of New Zealand history, coloured no less by its outlook than by the author's highly original personality. As much as *The Maori King* or, at the opposite pole, *Taranaki*, they reflect, though very subtly, the tense feelings which prevailed in the opening years of the wars.

Old New Zealand, the more personal of the two books, looks back in ostensibly unmethodical retrospection to the 'good old times' of the eighteen-thirties and contains mingled and not easily distinguished elements of biography and fiction.[23] It belongs, with important differences, to the class of pioneer memoirs, and in a superlative degree has the gusto and colloquial raciness (with a characteristic undertone of nostalgia) which lend charm and readability to the reminiscences of even the roughest literary diamond. Nowhere else in New Zealand literature is there anything to compare in force and humour with the account of Maning's arrival, or with the description, in the fourth chapter, of a plundering raid, to single out only two brilliant episodes from a possible dozen. As descriptive writer, as ironical commentator, as *raconteur*, Maning is unexcelled. But a close reading of *Old New Zealand* discloses the fact that its author, for all his air of casualness, is very far removed from the usual literary amateur of pioneer days. He is, in fact, the master of an art so skilled and so persuasive that it conceals the true nature of his aims and views. For Maning, it becomes evident, was by no means a simple seeker after truth like Gorst; rather was he acting the part of showman, concerned to paint the high lights and the low lights of savage life from a partisan point of view.

This is one explanation of the disproportionate emphasis he placed on warfare, an important but by no means all-absorbing part of the old order. The charge cannot be brought against the *War in the North*, where Maning confined himself to a single warlike episode in Maori history; but within the broader limits of *Old New Zealand* his selection of material is most significant. At least half the book, as a casual inspection of chapter-headings will show, is taken up with descriptions of war or its adjuncts, and scarcely a page is without some passing reference to fighting. True, in Maning's time, mainly through the introduction of the musket, the equilibrium of Maori culture had been disturbed so that warfare had assumed a tragically important role. Maning himself is a witness to the fact in some of the wisest and most penetrating sections of his book. But, invoking native authority, he goes much farther and states in a lurid passage that the same state of affairs existed before the coming of the European and the musket: 'Nothing was so valuable or respectable as strength and courage, and to acquire property by war and plunder [was] more honourable and also more desirable than by labour. Cannibalism was glorious. The island was a pandemonium.'[24] Such a distortion could, even in Maning's day, have been corrected by reference to the works of Grey and Shortland. A people engaged in a welter of senseless bloodshed could scarcely have preserved the qualities of mind and imagination revealed in Grey's three collections.

Even less understanding was shown in Maning's treatment of other native institutions. In his hands the *tapu* system was reduced to terms of insane melodrama, the *muru* to low comedy. Indeed the Maori of *Old New Zealand* is a creature alternating between farce and melodrama, witness two descriptions of the *tohunga*: 'He was an old, grave, stolid-looking savage, with one eye, the other had been knocked out long ago in a fight before he turned parson . . . a ferocious old cannibal, wizard, sorcerer, high priest, —as it appeared very probable,—to Satan himself.'; 'a stout athletic savage, with a countenance disgustingly expressive of cunning and ferocity, and who, as he stealthily marked me from the corner of his eye, I recognised as one of those limbs of Satan, a Maori *tohunga*.'[25]

On the positive side, Maning was at his best in describing those features of Maori life which he could be expected to comprehend and sympathize with—warfare and its attendant ceremonial, the elaborate processes of trade, the scene and ritual of death. The unmarred excellence of the *War in the North*, an account of the Flagstaff war, is largely due to its being confined within the limits of such material. The narrative, which is placed in the mouth of a Maori combatant, seems to have gained in precision and picturesqueness from Maning's knowledge of Maori oratory, while the monologue form gave him scope for ironical comment on Maori bewilderment at the incomprehensible ways of the European and on European misconceptions of the native. As a fighting man the Maori possessed virtues that were well within Maning's compass, and in the battle scenes his narrative skill was blended with imaginative sympathy to produce an effect that is reminiscent of the best prose translations of Homer. Even the *tohunga*, as he casts his omens at the beginning of the war, is a dignified figure, presented with no suggestion of ridicule. In this scene and in the greater part of the book, Maning shows an understanding and a power of self-projection notably absent from most of *Old New Zealand*. The undue praise lavished on the latter can perhaps be ascribed to its more blatant qualities; in its own day one source of its appeal undoubtedly lay in its implied view of the Maoris. Maning's English sponsor, the Earl of Pembroke, commented, 'The bubble of Maori civilization has burst. . . . The true level of the Maori, intellectually and morally, has become tolerably well known; moreover, his numbers are diminishing year by year.'[26]

Gold-mining, the third disruptive episode of this period, produced the smallest quantity of literature. It was perhaps too brief in duration and too cataclysmic in effect to throw up its equivalent of Chamier or Maning. In any case, the urban public of New Zealand was neither large enough nor distant enough to wish for vicarious experience of the gold-fields. Apart from brief episodes in the works of pastoral novelists like Bathgate or Ferguson, literature of the diggings consists of a few trivial romances and some rough yarns and memoirs set down in old age or stimulated by illusory ambitions for money and fame. The nearest approach to a local Bret Harte was B. L. Farjeon, whose *Shadows on the Snow* (1865?) is a feeble *Outcasts of Poker Flat* drowned in sentiment of Dickensian origin. Farjeon left New Zealand to become a writer of popular fiction and the founder of a literary family, his successor as novelist of the gold-fields being Vincent Pyke, author of *Wild Will Enderby* (1873) and *The Adventures of George Washington Pratt* (1874). These books, which enjoyed in their day a local and Australian popularity, are simple concoctions of melodrama and knock-about farce, moving inexorably to the climax of gold discovery and the finale of marriage. The heroes, embodying the miners' standards of appearance and conduct, are of great physical strength, aggressively independent and uncouth in manner, yet chivalrous in their treatment of women and strict in their adherence to the unwritten code of the gold-fields. The quintessence of the type is Pratt, the American backwoodsman who strides exuberantly through the two novels, dispensing rude justice, chewing his quid, and making oracular observations in exaggerated Americanese. In addition to the crimes of robbery and murder, villainy is chiefly a matter of dissipation beyond the demands of good-fellowship or, more serious, the underhand exploitation of another miner's 'strike'.

The writings of Farjeon and Pyke make wearisome reading today not so much because they are crude but because they are crude in the wrong way: the miners' idiom is largely ignored, and characters are made to speak either in luscious journalese or in the language of fifth-rate drama; for the humour of the gold-fields is substituted a heavy jocosity, expressing itself in such terms as, 'a region, the atmosphere of which is popularly supposed to be excessively sultry'; and over all is spread a thick treacle of sentimentality.[27] A little of the true savour of gold-mining days does, however, survive in certain fugitive books or, more often, pamphlets which can sometimes be met with in the larger New Zealand collections. In particular, Henry Lapham's *We Four* (1880), the record of an evening spent in capping yarns, bears upon it the marks of authenticity. The yarns are set down in free colloquial English, they are flavoured with salty male humour, and sweetened with that genuine sentiment which grew out of the stresses and privations of life in Otago and Westland. The longest of the four sketches, 'A Member of the Force,' is completely adult in its presentation of complex human behaviour and in its avoidance of either sentimentality or cynicism. At a lower level there are W. Davidson's *Stories of New Zealand Life* (1889), with their revelation of the miners' wild extravagance, and *Frank Melton's Luck* (1891) by Thos. Cottle, a redoubtable figure who strewed his pages with homely aphorisms in rugged but forceful language. ' "As long as a man earns what he wants on the square, and pays his way, we don't care a rap whether he is a member of Parliament, or So-and-so's bullock-driver." '[28] Thus asserts one of his characters; and the sentiment would have been cheered to the echo on every claim from Coromandel to Gabriel's Gully.

In the best of the memoirs, *Up and Down; or, Fifty Years' Colonial Experiences . . . being the Life History of Capt. W. J. Barry. Written by Himself . . .* (1879), there is the same vigour and slangy picturesqueness of speech, with the same background of hard living, robust pleasures, and single-minded pursuit of gold or money. Capt. Barry, like Thos. Cottle, was one of those gargantuan characters appropriate to an age which roasted its bullocks whole and dug out its gold by the shovelful. With the same aplomb with which he turned his hand to every occupation, from authorship to auctioneering, he met the mingled smiles and blows of an erratic fortune. He won wealth by hard work or speculation, only to lose it on the racecourse or to dissipate it in the pursuit of some misty legacy. At each rumour of gold discovery he sped from continent to continent, borrowing the passage money, if need be, from employer or friend. Finally we leave him, battered but indomitable, lecturing to the populace of Great Britain on the advantages of New Zealand as a field for colonization. The narrative is set down in a breathless, tumultuous style, with no trace of artifice or hint of selection; the account of his second wife's death, for example, takes up about a quarter of the space assigned to an anecdote on the marketing of chilblain ointment to frost-bitten gold-miners. If some New Zealand novelist should wish to re-create life on the gold-fields in all its extravagant diversity, he would find an abundance of raw material in this odyssey of a colonial adventurer.

The conditions in which so fantastic a person as Barry could flourish also gave rise to the spectacular career of Julius Vogel, a journalist who, swept, like Barry, to Otago by the gold-rushes, eventually became the most influential politician of his time. More than any other single person, Vogel was responsible for transmitting to the mainstream of New Zealand life what may be called the 'digger spirit', that mixture of optimism, chivalry, speculative daring, and opportunism which characterized the miner on the fields of Otago and Westland. At the end of his political career, while living in England, Vogel set down a kind of oblique testament of faith in *Anno Domini 2000; or, Woman's Destiny* (1889). Here, in all their resplendence, were the ideals he had laboured to impose on a generally acquiescent population.

The book is primarily a fantasy, an elaborate product of the mechanism underlying the dreams of wealth and power, of garish residences and over-dressed women, which are occasionally inserted in the gold-miners' yarns. But Vogel's dream is on a far more opulent scale, and it is further enriched by the inclusion of his favourite theories of politics and empire. The novel was written, an epilogue explains, first to show that the recognized dominance of either sex was unnecessary, secondly to advocate the formation of a unified British Commonwealth, thirdly to suggest the abolition of poverty by raising the standard of living. The action takes place in the year 2000 when the author's theories have long been in practice. There now exists a great British Commonwealth, led by women (for 'woman has become the guiding, man the executive, force of the world.'), while want has been abolished in all countries through the intervention of philanthropic capitalists.[29]

Three main strands of thought and sentiment run through this extravaganza, as indeed through the later history of New Zealand. Of the first, imperialism, Vogel was one of the country's most vociferous exponents. But coupled with a faith in the imperial destiny, there is evident a marked feeling of inferiority before the power and prestige of Britain, a feeling that finds its outlet in a form of compensation. Vogel looks forward to a time when the colonies will dictate British policy, when the Emperor will woo a New Zealander, when London will be only an historic appendage of the Empire. These two opposing sentiments—affection for the mother country and a desire to be free of her trammels—provide a key to the understanding of literary and social history in the next few decades. Equally prophetic, but also rooted in the past, were Vogel's humanitarian views, the natural outcome of nineteenth-century liberalism in the forcing conditions of the gold-field and the pioneering settlement. With the dawn of the year 2000, the world has become convinced: 'First,

That labour or work of some kind was the only condition of general happiness. Second. That every human being was entitled to a certain proportion of the world's good things. Third. That, as the capacity of machinery and the population of the world increased production, the theory of the need of labour could not be realized unless with a corresponding increase of the wants of mankind. . . . .'[30] Thus, on the eve of the nineties, were foreshadowed the principles of its social legislation, in fact of future New Zealand democracy. The remaining characteristics may be lumped under the heading of materialism. The novel abounds in vulgar scenes of wealth and in ostentatious settings, and the prodigality of titled characters also expresses a childish conception of human life and progress. Progress, for Vogel, consisted mainly in the accumulation and limited distribution of wealth and in the perfecting of machinery. Typically, he indulges in an orgy of mechanical speculation: in the year 2000 dictaphones are in general use, electricity and compressed air are available to all, air-cruisers reach New Zealand from Melbourne in sixteen hours.

Anno Domini 2000, with its tawdry ideals and commonplace sentiments, forms a monument not only to its author but to the 'gilded' years of New Zealand history, a time of optimism and grandiose speculation, when the possibilities of expansion seemed unlimited. Vogel's effervescent 'Progression, progression, always progression, has been the history of the centuries . . . .' would have been questioned by few New Zealanders, and the mere word 'future' in contemporary writings can be counted on to release a burst of windy rhetoric.[31] There remained, however, a few incorruptible spirits who had crossed the seas in quest not of riches but of the New Jerusalem. A speech of FitzGerald's, made during the years of Vogel's ascendancy, can be regarded as the epitaph of the 'old identity' pushed aside by the 'new iniquity' in its ardour for gold and progress: 'Gentlemen, I conclude this . . . discourse by entering my humble protest against the sacrifice of public honour and dignity to private wealth and luxury; by entering my protest against the vices of an age which subordinates its love of the beautiful to its worship of wealth; which prefers false glitter to true taste; which makes Art the advertisement of riches instead of their crown and glory; which wears false hair, false jewels, false gold; which makes one storied houses look like two storied houses; whose tastes and whose arts are essentially vain and selfish.'[32]

In the bustling pioneer years, it was inevitable that the arts should suffer some eclipse. As Samuel Butler said, it did not do 'to speak about John Sebastian Bach's "Fugues", or pre-Raphaelite pictures' to the settlers of Canterbury. Even those writers who seem, at this distance of time, to have been wholly at one with their environment could be despised for pursuing aims which to the practical man were unprofitable or absurd. Take Dugald Ferguson's advice to the local poet, given in his embittered old age: ' "Pray who do you think seriously regards those verses. . . ? Assume, instead of your wonted look of dreamy abstraction, a keen business or even money-grabbing expression. Instead of poetic visions, let your mind be absorbed by plans for the best mode of growing turnips. . . . Marry some cockatoo's daughter with . . . cows for her dowry. . . . Let your stockyard, knee-deep in dung, be the practical witness of your prosperity . . . . if you will follow this advice, you may make some headway in the world, besides securing the substantial respect of all around you as a man of shrewd sense, which regard for you at present they certainly have not.'[33]

But this neglect was not wholly due to the soullessness of a money-grabbing public; a share of blame must fall on the writers themselves. In the young poet, with his look of 'dreamy abstraction' and his 'poetic visions', Ferguson has embodied only too well the conception of the poetic that was current throughout this period. At the outset it can be illustrated from the *Poems* (1861) of the Canterbury settler C. C. Bowen:

> *From life's stern battle and its cares set free,*
> *Methought my spirit wandered far away,*
> *And for a time put off mortality*
> *Amid the groves of Helicon to stray:—*
> *I dreamt of heroes of a by-gone day,*
> *And many a bard and many a demi-god.* . . .[34]

Thirty years later the idea implied in these verses—that poetry was not concerned with the struggles and cares of daily life but with the remote, the insubstantial, the 'beautiful'—was given explicit expression by another writer of verse, D. W. M. Burn. 'The greatest function of the bard,' he wrote, '. . . is to sing . . . of what he sees when gazing awestruck into the deep chasmic secrets of the Universe.' This power was necessarily granted to few, but a lesser bard might perform a lower though still worthy function: 'The flowers, the trees, the birds, the sky, the sea, the hues of sunset, form a continual feast of beauty for his soul: and oftentimes he strings his lute and sings of them; and men awake in wonderment to the glory of the world they live in.'[35]

This was the theory of poetry commonly practised during the most strenuous years of New Zealand history and by men who were themselves actively engaged in the clearing of bush, the subjugation of Maoris, the mining of gold. That poetry might conceivably have some relation to these activities, that it might on occasion concern itself with turnips, cockatoos, and stockyards did not occur to these writers, caught as they were in the toils of the romantic tradition. Consider, for example, Frederick Napier Broome, the gay, energetic, resourceful F—— of Lady Barker's books. When he took up his pen and began to versify, it was not to write of the exhilarating life of a Canterbury squatter, but to indulge in such feeble imitations of the rhythm and imagery of Swinburne as in this exotic of *Poems from New Zealand* (1868):

Being, and manifold mother, laid upon life like a dream,
Fleeing to thee for another, a mightier thought and a theme,
. . . . .
Take me to thy beautiful bosom, thy bountiful breast,
Make it bare to the exquisite blossom, suckle me there with the
  rest. . . .[36]

Or, again, turn to that dusty epic, *Ranolf and Amohia* (1872), by Alfred Domett, leading spirit of the Nelson settlement, experienced civil servant and politician, the 'passionate fiery nature, full of suppressed energy, as proud as Lucifer' of Thomas Arnold's memoirs.[37] Yet how little of this has crept into the interminable cantos of his 'South-Sea Day-Dream', how little, in fact, of the New Zealand Domett himself had known and had helped to build in thirty years of strenuous public life! But, as he suggests in a set of prefatory verses, Domett as poet was leaving behind the New Zealand of struggling settlements, of sheep-farming, of gold discovery, of political brawls and native wars; he was ignoring all this to create a New Zealand fit for romantic poets to dream in:

> *From our Life of realities—hard—shallow-hearted,*
> *Has Romance—has all glory idyllic departed—*
>   *From the workaday World all the wonderment flown?*
> *Well, but what if there gleamed, in an Age cold as this,*
> *The divinest of Poets' ideal of bliss?*
> *Yea, an Eden could lurk in this Empire of ours,*
> *With the loneliest love in the loveliest bowers?*—[38]

This Eden, reconstructed with enormous pains from the available sources, was the New Zealand of pre-colonization years, a land of virgin forest populated by Maoris still immune from the influences of European civilization. But for all his diligent research, for all his laborious pictures of silica terraces, geysers, primeval forests, and what not, there is little more vitality in the epic than there is in Wilson's *Ena* or White's *Te Rou* which in substance it so closely resembles. Canto after canto is ground out in the same tedious manner, description succeeds description with a deadening prolixity, and the poem is finally crushed by the enormous weight of speculation placed on the trivial plot. The verse comes to life only when it felicitously echoes one of Domett's models; for example, in the Wordsworthian

> *Such sights and sounds inspired the growing Boy*
> *With wondering exultation and the joy*
> *Of deeper thought and loftier feeling lent*
> *To the mere gladness of temperament.*[39]

Or again when Domett draws on personal and deeply-felt experience, as he appears to have done in describing Ranolf's yearning for civilization:

> *It was the crave for intellectual food,*
> *For which a young enthusiast Thinker pines,*
>
> . . . . .
>
> *Ambition—progress—all the hope and pride*
> *Of true Existence seemed to him denied.*
> *That land so rich in Beauty's sensuous smile*
> *Seemed for the Soul, only a desert Isle.*[40]

These, however, are frail saplings in a forest of dead timber. *Ranolf and Amohia* is the supreme vagary of the romantic impulse in New Zealand; the pity is that a man of Domett's intelligence and experience should have turned his literary ambitions into so unprofitable a channel. There can be few readers who would not gladly exchange Domett's 'epic' for one brief volume of memoirs written with the unstudied eloquence of his diaries and correspondence.

The popular versifier of these years was not Bowen nor Broome nor Domett, but Bracken, whose writings enjoyed a vogue not since equalled in New Zealand and whose *Musings in Maoriland*, published in the jubilee year of 1890, with a dedication to Lord Tennyson, set the seal upon his reputation as national poet. Bracken was something of a 'character', a very mild version of Captain Barry. Born in Ireland, he migrated as a child to Australia, where he was in turn farm-boy, chemist's assistant, station-hand, shearer. He crossed over to Otago in the late eighteen-sixties and there found his niche in journalism, an occupation varied by excursions into politics. On one occasion he relieved the monotony of a debate by singing a comic song to the House, and as 'Paddy Murphy' he acquired fame for his comments on the 'goins on' of 'Parliment' written in doggerel Irish.[41] This was Tom Bracken, journalist and politician—a very different person from Thomas Bracken, poet. For the moment he began to woo 'the divine maiden—POESY' (to quote his own phrase), Bracken forgot politics, forgot humour, forgot the world about him, to weave together those doleful platitudes and flowery banalities which make up the greater part of his verse.[42] These lines, from a poetical address recited by him at the opening of a theatre, illustrate his conception of POESY:

> *Welcome, Thalia and Melpomene,*
> *Unto this fair White City by the sea!*
> *Behold! Apollo here has found a shrine*
> *Where his companions—all the Sacred Nine—*
> *May revel in harmonious glee. . . .*[43]

To do him justice, Bracken rarely sank to the level of such inflated fustian, and at his best he has some of Longfellow's knack of expressing the plain man's thoughts about life and death and love in simple measures and apt phrases. Nevertheless, except for superficial verbal differences, the ornate bulk of *Musings in Maoriland* might have been produced by any minor versifier in any part of the English-speaking world during the late nineteenth century. And the same may be said of the mass of New Zealand verse of this period. One meets with minor felicities of rhythm and phrase, sincere tributes to natural beauty, the worthiest of sentiments. But the writers seem to have no vital connexion with the life about them, they rarely stray from the conventional paths of romantic verse, and even more rarely discard romantic *clichés* to use the language of everyday speech. Occasionally in humorous verse, as in these lines from *Colonial Couplets* (1889) by G. P. Williams and W. P. Reeves, it is recognized that in fifty years New Zealand had developed an idiom of its own, very different from that of English people and English poets:

> *Then there's what we call a* gully, *which of course we take to mean*
> *Just a small and narrow valley, in which bush is sometimes seen;*
> *You perchance, were you a new chum, might describe this as a dell,*
> Bushy gully *suits me better, serves my purpose just as well;*
> Bush, *too, means the native forest; you will never, I'm afraid,*
> *Hear a self-respecting bushman call a bush a leafy glade. . . .*[44]

Even here the attitude is rather equivocal, as if the authors did not altogether approve the ousting of the poetic English term by its crude colonial equivalent. Not for many years were New Zealand writers to use their own language seriously and with self-assurance.

V

The Nineties

IN the next clearly defined phase of New Zealand history, roughly bounded by the nineties, certain marked tendencies may be discerned, arising from a situation that is simply stated. It was now half a century since the beginning of organized colonization, and pioneering (with important qualifications), gold-rushes, Maori wars were receding into the past. In the South Island and older settled parts of the North the population, swelled by the Vogel immigrant and the gold-miner turned settler, was subsiding into comparative stability. By the beginning of the period, small farmers and urban workers had displaced the squatters with their satellites as the dominant class, and had elected a government to give legislative expression to their needs and aspirations. Wealth, won from gold and refrigeration, had brought with it increased leisure, and both wealth and leisure were soon to be distributed more evenly by the new code of laws.

The easier conditions of life gave rise to what André Siegfried, the acutest observer of the period, was to term *'le snobisme'*: in his own words, 'The first settlers were modest, unpretentious people . . . their first care was to gain their living, and, as they had left Europe without hoping to return, they were but little affected by the thousand petty vanities of older societies. Later on the Colony became organized into a regular society, and the New Zealanders, formerly pioneers, became what are known to-day as *colonials*. . . . Wealth came to them at the same time; there was general ease; society (in the narrow sense) began to flourish and to show less indifference to hierarchies and honours.'[1]

On the other hand, there were stirrings of art and literature, chiefly among a small group of colonial-born men and women, romantically aware of their unique place as the first generation of a new state. 'We stand in the parting of the ways,' announced one of their spokesmen in 1899. 'The young scion of New Zealand national life has begun to awake to a knowledge of itself.'[2] The clarion call was, in fact, a little belated. For by 1899 the force of the movement was largely spent, and the most distinguished member of the new generation, William Pember Reeves, had left for England, thus choosing his 'way' which was, generally speaking, to be the way for the next thirty years.

Reeves's career touched almost every side of the New Zealand of his day. The son of a well-to-do Canterbury public man, he was a pupil at Christ's College, and then, following the custom among the more privileged at the time, was sent to Oxford to complete his education. Ill health soon brought him back to New Zealand, where he took up law, journalism, and politics on the Liberal side. At the age of thirty he entered Parliament, becoming a member of the first Liberal–Labour Cabinet. As Siegfried was quick to recognize, Reeves was the intellect behind the new legislation. It was he who formulated the code of industrial laws and devised the machinery of arbitration. And in his record as Minister of Education there are signs of a realization that this work was only a prelude, a necessary adjustment of social and economic conditions before the higher aims of an enlightened democracy were pursued. For Reeves was more than mere politician and social reformer; he was a man of culture, 'a brilliant and easy writer, a talented man of letters, and an occasional poet' (to quote from Siegfried's eulogy).[3] In *State Experiments in Australia and New Zealand* (1902) he gave the new nation a record of its achievements as a social laboratory; in *The Long White Cloud* (1898) he wrote its history with an easy charm that made it accessible to every citizen; in *New Zealand* (1898) he supplied it with a national song, proclaiming in resonant phrases pride in its natural setting:

> *God girt her about with the surges,*
> *And winds of the masterless deep....*

pride in its democratic and equalitarian principles:

> *Though little and latest their nation,*
> *Yet this they have won without sword,*

> *That woman with man shall have station,*
> *The toiler be lord.*

pride in its humanitarianism:

> *Where pity worn age shall environ*
> *Where the young start abreast in their race.* ....[4]

In his 'occasional' poetry (a just description of his minor but accomplished and historically interesting verses), Reeves dramatized an issue which constantly recurs in the literature of the nineties. The New Zealander of 'A Colonist in His Garden' has opened a letter from an English friend who describes the mellow beauties of England, with its opportunities for a richer, ampler life, and urges him to leave those

> '*Isles nigh as empty as their deep,*
> *Where men but talk of gold and sheep*
> *And think of sheep and gold.*
> *A land without a past; a race*
> *Set in the rut of commonplace.* ....'

Reeves's ideal colonial self refutes these criticisms:

> '*No art?*' *Who serves an art more great*
> *Than we, rough architects of State*
> *With the old earth at strife?*[5]

and elects to remain in the colony. This was the literary decision. In fact, Reeves left New Zealand in 1896, 'at once,' according to Siegfried, 'found himself very much at his ease in the most cultured circles in London,' and established himself there for the remainder of his life.[6]

Reeves was the intellectual leader of the new generation; its spiritual representative, the mouthpiece of its troubled adolescent soul, was Jessie Mackay, a native of Canterbury like Reeves. The unassuming preface to *The Spirit of the Rangatira*, published in 1889, when she was twenty-five years of age, contains the first clear signs of national self-awareness. 'I am convinced,' she wrote, 'that the heart of young New Zealand, in these days, beats with the free, untrammelled pulsation of enterprise ... and, side by side with this aspiration after culture goes the dawning of a national spirit. ...'[7] In this collection of ballads and in *The Sitter on the Rail* (1891) it is not always easy to disentangle the national spirit from the expression of Jessie Mackay's own decided views or from the Gaelic romanticism which she drew from her Scottish parentage and a wide range of reading. Hers, at any rate, is the voice of impetuous youth, burning with indignation at injustice and oppression, full of pity for the weak, scornful of both compromise and clogging common sense—a voice that is raised again, more stridently, in the feminist novels of the period. Ranging through history and her own Scottish heritage, she sang the praises of men and women who had lived and died for a cause—Hannibal, Charlotte Corday, Gordon, Henare Taratoa of Gate Pa, obscure figures of Scottish or Scandinavian legend. Her faith is proclaimed succinctly in 'For Conscience' Sake', where the speaker, who has chosen duty rather than love, asserts:

> *It was better all as it was;*
> *That severed our ways should be on earth,*
> *All for a noble cause. ...*[8]

With this lofty idealism is combined the humanitarian sentiment of the time, expressed in pity for oppressed nations and minorities or in gloomy reflections on the inequalities of society and the sufferings of the poor. Her vision of 'the Earth with all her thousand wrongs' in 'A Vision' typifies the somewhat jaundiced social conscience of the new generation, or at least of its more articulate members:

> *Some bled beneath a rusty chain;*
> *And some were lapped in eiderdown;*
> *And one in sackcloth hid his pain;*
> *Another wore a golden crown.*[9]

Most of the poems are about remote themes and people dead and gone. When her vision is focused nearer home and the 'cause' is presented in terms of prohibition and women's rights, the effect is often incongruous, and the verse sheds its heroic glamour. She cared for these causes intensely, even passionately, yet as poetic material they proved intractable in her hands. For at heart Jessie Mackay was an inveterate romantic, and, as with most of her generation, her allegiance was uneasily divided between the world of her parents and her native country. Alan Mulgan has written, 'It is significant that her most thrilling experience when she visited the Old World was her visit to the ruins of Tintagel....'[10] Though later, in 'The Noosing of the Sun-God', she was to write one of the few successful verse renderings of Maori myth, at this period her Scottish peasants carry greater conviction than her Maoris, and she is more at home in Scandinavian mythology than in Polynesian. Courageous, sincere, high-minded, but as poet striving to give voice to a national spirit that was hardly yet in being, Jessie Mackay belongs in native New Zealand literature to that 'little gray company before the pioneers' which was to form the subject of her best-known poem.[11]

The change which occurred in New Zealand letters with Pember Reeves and Jessie Mackay is even more pronounced in the novels of the nineties. These also mark the advent of colonial-born writers and with them departures from the hitherto dominant plot of emigration and pioneering. The remittance man and other stock figures of pioneer fiction, though they never wholly disappear, occur with less monotony, and themes emerge which indicate a people beginning tentatively—and often clumsily enough—to concern itself with the finer issues of living. Most of the novels, it is worth noting, were written by women; for women remained the chief diffusers of 'light', while the pioneer convention of a hard-headed, horny-handed masculinity continued to prevail.

Edith Searle Grossmann, the most ambitious of the novelists, was one of those early graduates of the University of New Zealand whose zeal and sense of apostleship, often combined with considerable—and ill-digested—erudition, had an appreciable influence on this decade. Her three earliest books were uncompromisingly didactic in purpose, avowed weapons in the militant feminist campaign. 'The following narrative,' runs a note in the third, 'is based on a study from the past, before the Woman Movement had raised the conditions of women; and it is produced now in view of a strong reactionary tendency towards re-subjection.' The crudely immature *Angela: A Messenger* (1890) illustrates, chiefly by implication, the narrow background of domestic life and Protestant nonconformity from which, as Siegfried noted, the allied feminist and prohibition movements derived their peculiar strength. *In Revolt* (1893) and its sequel, *A Knight of the Holy Ghost* (1907), belong to a later and more aggressive stage of the campaign, whose perfervid atmosphere may be suggested by a typical passage: 'Ah, those early days of a great movement! Who can bring back in later years the same intensity of life, the hope and faith, the enthusiasm we feel in thinking we see the redemption of the world coming visibly and by our hands? ... To work, to suffer, and to rejoice for some great object—to Hermione this meant happiness. All her days were steeped in the rich after-glow that follows the renunciation of personal life.'[12] It is easy to recognize how such a movement took the form of a crusade, and indeed Hermione, the persecuted heroine of these two novels, surrounded by her neophytes and finally driven to a violent death, has all the attributes of a martyr, even of a Messiah.

The feminist movement did not arise without reason, and in the colonial setting of the novels it is possible to trace some of its local origins. Hermione's husband is a wealthy Australian farmer, popular and ostentatiously generous, but coarsened by an indulgent upbringing and the primitive life on his station—a life which the author depicts with horrified fascination: 'Then he had some foals broken in, and she saw him cutting at them while the blood streamed from their gashes. He was swearing brutally and shouting, yet she thought bitterly he seemed in his element.'[13] The climax comes when, in a fit of drunken dementia, he murders their eldest child. Except for one tranquil episode in a European setting (devoted in the best feminist manner to prolonged debates on philosophy, religion, and art), the books contain a succession of similar horrors. But they are not those of 'synthetic' melodrama, where a plot is deliberately manipulated to tantalize an audience; they belong rather to a kind of 'raw' melodrama, which is based on genuine experience yet not assimilated into the reasoned scheme of tragedy. It is evident that the author was a woman of refinement and education. Certainly no desire for notoriety or success based on a spurious 'frankness' impelled her to disregard the taboos of an outwardly puritanical society by writing of drunkenness and the rest. It was as if the emotional disorders of the pioneer years, occasionally hinted at by a writer like Chamier, had in this generation and in this woman welled up to demand expression. Naturally, too, she was concerned with social reform, women's rights, the vote; for these were the remedies which presented themselves to a politically minded age.

The literature of prohibition seldom reaches the moral heights of Mrs. Grossmann's novels. In one of Jessie Mackay's later poems, 'Vigil,' the movement takes on the dignity of a struggle between the forces of good and evil:

> O my land, do you hear
> The pure Presences pray
> For your life, for your soul?
> Is it 'Yea'; is it 'Nay,'
> For your life, for your soul?[14]

And Kathleen Inglewood's novel *Patmos* (1905) occasionally reflects the same religious exaltation as well as the rare virtue of humour. But more typical is a spirit of illiberal self-righteousness showing all the narrowness with none of the compensating depth of the traditions represented by *The Pilgrim's Progress* and *The Scarlet Letter*. The novels are tracts in fictional guise, stuffed with trite moral tags, often taking the form of those gross texts once exported in bulk from America, and their prose is the merest tissue of *clichés*. If they show any development, it is a steady decline from the vigorous opening years of the cause to the time when it had become a matter of political lobbying and nation-wide propaganda.

Ko Meri or A Cycle of Cathay (1890) by Jessie Weston occupies an intermediate position between the fiction of causes and Lady Wilson's two novels of New Zealand 'polite' society. Its setting is a comfortable suburb of Auckland, where women occupy themselves in running households, paying calls, painting water-colours, and gossiping, much as they would have done in any English provincial town at about the same time. Yet they are provincials very remote from their centre, London, whither, as the author observes, their thoughts 'ever gravitate' as 'the Mecca of the race'. For them the visit of an English cousin, with his news of 'relations at "home" ', is an event to cause flutterings and heart-burnings and to be celebrated by an endless round of picnics and parties, while the return trip to England is not to be undertaken unless after lengthy counsels and elaborate preparation. But there are signs of a local independence. Two figures of mild fun are a headmaster and his wife, 'of course from England, facts which neither he nor his wife were likely to forget, nor allow anyone else to do so', and, contrasting with them, two New Zealand girls, 'both hyper-sensitive about disparaging remarks with regard to the Colonies'.[15]

The setting of the novel, however, is purely incidental. This suburban group forgathers not only for social pleasures but, in the manner of the nineties, for the discussion of politics, of social reform, and above all, of religion. *Robert Elsmere* looms oppressively in the background, and Mr. Everard, a broad Churchman, is a figure cut very close to Mrs. Humphry Ward's pattern. Prevented by doctrinal scruples from taking a parish, he is continually scourged by the thought of social evils and inequalities. He cannot enjoy the fresh beauty of New Zealand, for it serves only to remind him of ' "the thousands in Great Britain pining for fresh air and sunshine, cooped up in dense cities, and miserable always".' Then there is the half-caste Mary Balmain, sceptical about the conversion of her mother's people: ' "the form of religion appeals to their fancy; the spirit they are utterly unable to comprehend." ' With these are ranged other assorted types: Mary's guardian, the sincere agnostic; Lenore Dayton, the probing but pious intellectual; the rest of the Dayton family, passive, vegetable Christians, for whom church-going is merely a piece of social ritual; Mr. McLeod, the aesthete and hedonist, whose aestheticism takes the practical form of gardening. The story rarely moves far from the arena of religious discussion and closes with portentous hints of a second coming: 'Truly, the whole creation groaneth and travaileth!'[16]

Intertwined with the theme of religion are others more indigenous in character, the problem of the dying Maori and the conviction that the half-caste would inevitably return to his tribe. Mary Balmain, the heroine, is the daughter of an Englishman and a Maori woman, who had left the child in infancy to live with her own people. Mary's guardian has given her a cultured and liberal upbringing which, reinforced by her wealth, has qualified her to take a place in Auckland society. She mixes on equal terms with girls of her own age and, supreme triumph, wins the hand of a visiting English officer. But she feels herself to be one of a doomed race and constantly reiterates this belief. It needs only a personal disaster, the death of her fiancé, for her to lose her civilized veneer and return to her mother's tribe. To the entreaties of a friend she replies, ' "The night that has fallen upon my race has fallen upon me, and it is well that I should share the darkness with my own people. Before long the Maori will cease to stand in the path of the white man. . . . They are not adapted for that civilization which has taken the pakeha . . . hundreds of years to attain. . . ." '[17]

This conception of the Maoris as a people whose culture and possibly whose life were doomed to extinction was one widely prevalent in the nineties. It may have influenced the founders of the Polynesian Society in 1892, and it is certainly implicit in Augustus Hamilton's monumental *The Art Workmanship of the Maori Race in New Zealand*, publication of which began in 1896. As a literary theme it attracted many writers besides Jessie Weston. Jessie Mackay touched on it in 'The Spirit of the Rangatira', as she did on almost every problem of her time. With the half-caste theme, it was used by Harry B. Vogel in *A Maori Maid* (1898), a first novel more substantial than its title might suggest, showing a promise that was never fulfilled. Again it appeared in *Maoriland Stories* (1895) and *Tales of a Dying Race* (1901), those sardonic sketches of the Maoris by A. A. Grace, son of the Taupo missionary.

The dying Maori even penetrated the refuge of Anne Glenny Wilson's *Alice Lauder* (1893). In a rather implausible passage of small talk between two European visitors, one of them remarks, ' "They are a grand race of people in some ways, and what a tragedy it is to see them fading away, blighted by the mere touch of our civilization!" '[18] Such topics, however, seldom ruffle the polite surface of this and its companion piece, *Two Summers* (1900); the two novels are chiefly concerned with the recreations, the social customs, and the decorous love-making of the colonial gentry, exponents of Siegfried's 'snobisme'. This small group of landowners and professional people, heirs of the squattocracy, is admirably described in the author's own words: 'Alicia's circle and atmosphere had seemed to him hitherto too much and too consciously a copy of the English original; they were much the same as would be met in any smaller English centre, but tinned, as it were, and of rather provincial flavour at that.'[19] The description might also be applied to the novels themselves, which are colonial attempts at the comedy of manners. They contain a great deal of cultivated talk about music, society, art, but the poise is precarious and highly self-conscious. The pages are spattered with decayed French words and phrases—*noms de guerre, intime, mariage de convenance, affaire de coeur*—the insignia of an uncertain and uneasily assimilated culture. The characters do not exist in the social vacuum traditional in this kind of novel, but break through into the underworld of domestic cares and financial difficulties, or rise to the plane where people love in vain, where parents or children die and are mourned. And occasionally the writer forgets her English manner and, like any untutored colonial, writes rapturously of the scenery of her country—which she is yet never so indelicate as openly to name.

It is a curious hybrid world, this colonial *monde* of the nineties, and its local elements are thrown into relief when its members encounter their English prototypes, as they frequently do in these novels. ' "Well, as we were saying," [The visiting Englishman counsels his *inamorata*.] "if you use all your favourite expressions when you go to England, people will call you a *Colonial*. Think of that!" '[20] When the translation is effected, however, the comments on the master nation are often adversely critical and pungently expressed. Of the English social poise the author writes, 'It was the perfect understanding of an English county family of their own desirable situation in life, which gave them this effortless calm of demeanour, undisturbed by fruitless attempts at wit or entertainment.' On the delicacy of their palate she comments, 'As to the ordinary English mind the penalty of one day's cold soup is almost more than can be borne. . . .' And judging an English country-house by the standards of colonial domesticity, she concludes, 'Every corner of its wide expanse was warmed, and lighted, and watered, and ventilated, and waited on by some latent invention of art and science; and almost the only thing that could not be obtained by pressing a button, or turning a tap in every room in the house, was the sense of home.'[21]

These are signs that point to differences and mild antagonisms felt even by the class of New Zealanders who deliberately modelled their lives on the English pattern. For the literature of the nineties, like its legislation, is marked by a spirit of independence, owing something to the Australian national movement, but more often of local origin. Writers of the new generation were resolved to work out their own destiny—in what manner and against what handicaps may be judged by a glance at the *New Zealand Illustrated Magazine*. This was founded in 1899 by a group of university graduates and public men in response to an 'often-expressed desire amongst patriotic literary men and general readers to have a Magazine with a distinctive New Zealand colouring, one which will have for its aims the encouragement of the best Literary and Artistic Talent which we have in our midst. . . .'[22]

There is a melancholy interest in the early numbers of the *Illustrated*, with their eager theorizings about a national culture. New Zealand had come to the 'parting of the ways', so ran a manifesto in the first number. The self-consciousness of the nation had already asserted itself in 'the political sphere', but as yet its 'literary instinct' had been content to express itself through the forms of the old world. Still, the conditions for a literary renascence seemed 'peculiarly favourable'. New Zealand's pre-eminent natural beauty was there 'to train unconsciously eye and mind to a perception of the beautiful'. Her insular position favoured the development of a national type and 'that artistic creativeness which is the outcome of a strongly-impressed character'. She had a past 'not without its dangers and its honourable triumphs'.[23] She had been continuously in touch with a remote stage of human development. Two things were required before a native literature would burst into flower: a public educated to the possibilities of such a literature and a medium in which its creators could exercise their powers. These needs were to be met by the *New Zealand Illustrated*.

It will be seen that the *Illustrated* took a serious view of its functions, and despite the garishness of its cover and the general tastelessness of its format, the first volume makes a commendable showing. The chief defects are an academic adiposity in the articles and a flaccid sentimentality in the illustrations and verse. But the magazine soon lowered the exalted tone of its opening issues and degenerated into a popular review crammed with short stories, articles, snippets, selected—if they were selected—on principles of indulgent catholicity. If this were the wine of a new literature, one can only comment, it was being poured into oddly assorted bottles, many of them doubtful in quality. The only contributions of permanent value were articles on anthropology; and it is significant that of the many young writers represented in the *Illustrated*, few except the historians, the economists, and the anthropologists (among them James Hight, Elsdon Best, Guy H. Scholefield, James Cowan, and Johannes C. Andersen) were later to find a permanent niche in New Zealand letters. The country had a good deal to offer such writers, but little for aspiring poets and novelists.

What has been said of the *Illustrated* applies, in greater or less degree, to all the literature of the nineties and the adjacent years—to the work of Arthur H. Adams, once the hope and later the disappointment of New Zealand letters, to the confident rhymes of university students, to the verses of those who wrote in the shadow of Jessie Mackay. In all the writings of this generation, with the exception of Reeves's prose, there are signs of prematurity, as of people urgently striving to say something but without adequate means of self-expression. The writers were enthusiastic, often deeply in earnest, but they lacked poise and self-discipline. Moreover, they did not know enough. They theorized in terms of a local, 'indigenous' culture when expanding communications were abolishing, or at least modifying, that conception. They were prone to assume that the beauty of their surroundings would, spontaneously and without effort on their part, be reflected in their prose and verse. Their minds were immature, their work provincial in form and outlook. The fact was they lived in a society still inchoate. Unlike their fathers, they had not enjoyed the advantages of an upbringing in the old world, with its more stable traditions. The advantages of New Zealand were as yet of a different kind and not immediately helpful to young writers. So the literary movement petered out in frustration and indifference, and not until the nineteen-thirties was the clamour of nationalism heard again. For the next three decades literary New Zealand, like political and economic New Zealand, aspired only to be the most submissive offspring of the mother country. Throughout this period the legislation of the nineties grew in esteem, while the parallel literary movement was forgotten, or remembered only in the figures of Pember Reeves and Jessie Mackay.

VI
Years of Prosperity

IN 1910 Edith Searle Grossmann published her last novel, *The Heart of the Bush*. As its title suggests, it was a simple-seeming romance, placid in tone, restricted in setting, almost banal in plot —different in every way from the writer's earlier novels, with their nervous, sometimes hysterical, manner and violent situations. *The Heart of the Bush* reflects the calm temper of the years which succeeded the troubled nineties, and, possibly without the author's intention, it supplied a parable for those three expansive decades.

The heroine of the romance, Adelaide Borlase, is a New Zealander who, after being educated in England, returns to her father's home in the back country of Canterbury. In the first part of the novel, 'Between Two Hemispheres,' she is seen attempting to adapt her acquired English self to colonial ways and surroundings. ' "I feel that I am transmigrating and am a compound of two beings," ' she exclaims; and once the first mood of exhilaration is past, she finds the farm and all about it 'vulgar, jarring, lowest middle-class'. For relief she escapes to a neighbouring sheep station, where things are done in the English manner, where the men 'dress for dinner', and an appropriate decorum is observed. ' "It isn't very wicked to be impulsive, is it?" ' inquires Adelaide of one of this household. ' "It's un-English," said Evelyn, with soft condemnation, stifling like a down pillow.'[1]

The conflict finally resolves itself into a choice between two men, one a New Zealand-born farmer ('His patriotism was local and narrow, but it was intense. He loved these mountains and these valleys as the Celt and the Gael love their misty islands and craggy hills.'), the other an English nephew of the station-owner, sharply caricatured: 'He could not imagine any form of bliss for people who had no hope of ever getting to London.' This choice also involves one between the restricted lot of a small-farmer's wife and ease in the English microcosm of the wealthy, with periodic visits to England itself. Adelaide finally chooses the New Zealander. But the novel does not end here; a further conflict has yet to be resolved. Her husband wishes to give Adelaide the wealth and luxury she has sacrificed in marrying him, and, equipped as he is with brains and energy, he soon becomes the local magnate, the driving force behind a refrigeration plant and a dairy factory. Preoccupied with these affairs, he neglects his wife, but at length the two see the situation in its true perspective, and the man returns to that unambitious life of small-farming to which he is suited by inclination and temperament: 'Here he had been born, and here, if it had not been for his wife, he would have been content to do his life-work, and to die and be buried.'[2]

It is tempting to read this romance as a deliberate parable for the times. But whether or not it was conceived with didactic intention, *The Heart of the Bush* is of interest in showing the kind of themes which attracted a thoughtful woman who in her earlier novels had already discussed simpler problems. In some degree, these had been settled, and more intricate questions, occasionally voiced in the nineties, were becoming insistent as the years went on. What were to be the standards of the New Zealand people as they took possession of the comfortable dominion built by their own efforts and those of the pioneers? Would prosperity be used merely to acquire more prosperity and material fripperies, or would it supply the conditions for a more balanced manner of life than had hitherto been possible? It was the ancient choice between God and Mammon, or, substituting local symbols, between FitzGerald and Vogel. Closely related was a second question: Were the New Zealanders to continue in meek subservience to the standards of the old world, or should they essay the more difficult course of shaping their own life as a people?

Complex issues are perceived and dealt with more easily by novelists than by societies; and it is the constant, never-resolved interplay of these opposed principles that lends interest to what would otherwise be the most depressing period of New Zealand history. It would be broadly true to say that New Zealand made a choice directly contrary to the one Mrs. Grossmann imposed on her characters—that its people elected to pursue the phantom of prosperity and the vain ideal of 'more English than England' rather than accommodate themselves to their own surroundings. Such a conclusion would receive some support from the writings of those who visited the country in the wake of Siegfried. It is a conclusion fully documented in the ablest survey of the period, the last chapter of *New Zealand in the Making*, published in 1930, when the era of prosperity was drawing to a close, and written by J. B. Condliffe, himself a New Zealander. It is a conclusion which must be modified, however, not so much in the light of a number of small exceptions (important as they are), but because each of the 'two hemispheres' was in this period to provide the conditions for the flowering of a major talent. Katherine Mansfield found herself only by escaping from the suffocating materialism of New Zealand. In the heart of that same New Zealand, actively engaged in its main industry, Guthrie-Smith wrote *Tutira*.

One result of New Zealand's origins in the steamship age was that within fifty years of its foundation the voyage 'Home' had become an established institution. In the nineties it was accepted as such, and by 1907 it bulked so large that William Satchell made an overseas steamer the setting of a novel, *The Elixir of Life*. The passengers, who are returning by the Cape route, form a fairly typical group. There are a cabinet minister, a young physician who has gone abroad to gain experience, tourists in search of scenery or health, emigrants crowded into the steerage quarters, and 'colonists returning home from the long-anticipated European tour'.[3] Had the voyage been made in the opposite direction, the list would probably have included a writer, for from the time of B. L. Farjeon and Fergus Hume there had been a steady export of New Zealand talent which reached its greatest dimensions after the First World War.

The situation behind this drift to Europe was a complex one. There were cogent economic reasons why writers with ambitions beyond journalism should seek the publishing facilities and the wider audience lacking in New Zealand; only in fairly recent times has the local publication of fiction been common, and a

London imprint still has greater value in terms of cash and recognition. Again, writers sought in the old world surroundings more sympathetic and stimulating than those of New Zealand; they migrated to London, as Americans of the 'lost generation' migrated to Paris. Added to these were reasons the more powerful because they were intangible—reasons arising from the circumstances of New Zealand's foundation and its status as a colony. In the first years of its history the conception of a 'Brighter Britain' had already taken shape, and by the seventies Anthony Trollope was able to characterize the New Zealander as 'among John Bulls . . . the most John-Bullish'.[4] This imperial sentiment, fostered by successive political leaders and further strengthened during the Boer War and the First World War, culminated in the nineteen-twenties, when it found permanent expression in Alan Mulgan's *Home* (1927). To a reader unfamiliar with the local idiom, 'Home' might have been thought to refer to the writer's native country, since he had been born in New Zealand and had there grown to maturity. Such a misapprehension would have been quickly dispelled by a glance at the first chapter, where the word is defined at considerable length. The author mentions the powerful associations that gathered round it and describes the literary diet of his youth and manhood, concluding, 'The trend of all this literature, read desultorily and with no purpose, was to fix my thoughts ever on England. Nor do I suggest for a moment that my experience was unique or even exceptional.'[5]

No New Zealander who grew up in the years centred in the First World War would challenge the essential accuracy of this statement or its wide applicability. Education, reading, prevailing sentiment, economic interest—all turned the New Zealand writer's thoughts and ambitions towards England; and, given the opportunity, it was to England he migrated. 'To London The Dream and the Fulfilment,' so ran the dedication to a novel of this period.[6] A few of New Zealand's literary *émigrés* were to learn in the conditions of exile a new understanding of their country. But the greater number discarded the more obvious traces of their colonial origin, merged themselves in the English literary world, and devoted their talents to the cultivation of some current fashion in letters or to the glorification of those circles of English life which they had come to regard as enshrining the social absolute. Lacking well-defined standards, equipped with physical energy and sufficient if limited education, some of these writers were well qualified to succeed in journalism and the underworld of English letters, but neither their country's literature nor the world's has been notably enriched by their self-imposed exile. With few exceptions, the single ticket to England (as distinct from the return passage) has proved itself the entrance to a blind alley. It was in the old world, however, that New Zealand's most gifted imaginative writer found the conditions she needed for self-expression.

'New Zealand is in my very bones,' Katherine Mansfield once wrote, and the remark has a deeper meaning than she herself may have realized.[7] Born in Wellington in 1888, she was of the second colonial generation, the member of a family whose local history was almost coextensive with that of British New Zealand. In the late eighteen-forties her grandfather, Arthur Beauchamp, left England for the Australian gold-fields, where his career was adventurous and varied enough but, from a worldly point of view, unsuccessful. In 1860 he crossed to New Zealand, started an auctioneering business, took up with gusto the early-colonial sport of politics, and was at different times storekeeper, sawmiller, and government valuer. Like so many of his generation, Arthur Beauchamp was a 'character'—vigorous, enterprising, blessed with the pioneer gift for rhyming and the power to recite Byron 'for a solid hour and a half'—but erratic and unstable.[8] It was left for his colonial-born son, the father of Katherine Mansfield, to establish himself in the country and achieve solid material success. For a portrait of this self-made colonial magnate we need only turn to his daughter's work, where, under the name of Stanley Burnell, he is seen rising to a position of affluence which allowed him to confer on his daughters the advantages of an English education. Thus the Beauchamps had passed through the successive stages of New Zealand social history, from pioneering to a prosperity which made possible an ampler way of life, modelled on that of England.

After three years at Queen's College, London, Katherine Mansfield returned to New Zealand in 1906, but not, according to expectations, as a 'finished' young lady ready for the social round of New Zealand's capital city. She came back unwillingly, and, as a passage from one of her notebooks indicates, bringing with her alarming theories and ambitions: 'I should like to write a life much in the style of Walter Pater's *Child in the House*. About a girl in Wellington; the singular charm and barrenness of that place. . . . And then to leave the place and go to Europe. To live there a real existence—to go back and be utterly disillusioned, to find out the truth of all—to return to London—to live there an existence so full and so strange. . . .' This outpouring gives a hint of early reflections on the material of her best work and reveals the ambition dominating those adolescent years—to flee from the provincialism of Wellington, 'Philistia itself', and return to London; '*London*—it is Life' she wrote in her impassioned diary, echoing a thousand young New Zealand writers.[9] Finally, in 1909, she did return to England, from which point it is possible to trace from her published works the development of a talent that was to find its perfect material in the experiences of the New Zealand years.

Her first book, *In a German Pension* (1911), a series of sketches set in Bavaria, is immature work, crude in more than a technical sense, but interesting in its anticipation of themes and types which reappear in the later stories. The collection illustrates for the first time that intense interest in foreign scenes and people which is a marked but not always successful feature of her writings; she was here, as she remained even in so accomplished a story as 'Je ne parle pas Français', something of the colonial on tour, with a keen eye for the picturesque or the sordid in the life of 'those foreigners', and with a habit of judging them by the rigid standards of her own upbringing. Some of her foreign pictures are, however, unforgettable, and where there is lack of sympathy, as in this book, it is partly due to the ill health which usually took her to the Continent.

Contrasting with the slight sketches of *pension* life and the immature attempts at satire, there are two stories of greater substance, 'A Birthday' and 'The-Child-Who-Was-Tired'. The first, in spite of a camouflage of German names, is clearly an early attempt to handle the characters and scenes of 'Prelude' and the other New Zealand stories. Stanley Burnell appears, under the label of 'Andreas Binzer', invoking 'the government' in characteristic New Zealand terms, and moving against a background that is undisguised and unmistakable. The picture of Binzer peering with disgust into a 'gully', filled with empty tins and fennel, and, as a result, composing 'a letter to the papers', is one that fits with ease into the New Zealand landscape, though scarcely into the Bavarian.[10] The grandmother, the wife, the servant-girl are lightly but recognizably sketched, and we are introduced to the close intimacy of the New Zealand home, with its emotional cross-currents and small antagonisms. The main theme—the conflict between sensitive wife and domineering husband, so much more subtly handled in 'At the Bay'—is one that links Katherine Mansfield with the novelists of the nineties and may, in part, be derived from their common pioneer or near-pioneer background.

'The-Child-Who-Was-Tired', like the later 'Life of Ma Parker' and 'Miss Brill', may also owe something to a colonial or, rather, democratic sympathy with the underdog; an observant and sensitive child could not live through the humanitarian nineties without breathing in some of its prevailing sentiment. What is certain, however, is that the story provides the earliest evidence of Katherine Mansfield's knowledge of Chekhov. Interpreted by John Middleton Murry as presenting 'a symbol of her experience of life', 'her first effort to translate that experience into the forms of art', 'The-Child-Who-Was-Tired' is, in fact, a version of Chekhov's story 'Sleepy'.[11] She did not again attempt so close an imitation of the Russian master (though the unfinished 'A Married Man's Story' is a remarkable *tour de force* reminiscent of his manner), but through his example she was helped to a solution of her problems as a writer and a person.

The work of the next eight years, posthumously collected in *Something Childish* (1924), begins with a group of New Zealand stories which seem to have occupied her during the years between 1910 and 1912. Three of them, 'The Woman at the Store,'

'Millie,' and 'Ole Underwood' are nearer approaches to what is usually expected of the colonial author than anything else she wrote. The settings are primitive, the characters uncouth, the plots appropriately melodramatic. The men, like those of other sensitive women writers (Robin Hyde has several examples), are uncompromisingly male, their female counterparts are little more complex, while both sexes speak and think in a bucolic dialect which only an educated person could have conceived. This was an aspect of New Zealand she was ill equipped to treat and wisely abandoned. In the two remaining items of this group, 'New Dresses' and 'The Little Girl', she is seen approaching her true *métier*, the short story of childhood and adolescence based on her own memories: these, in fact, are the main links between 'A Birthday' and 'Prelude'. In technique, in the handling of material, they mark a decided advance on the earlier work, and there is a related development in the range of sympathies and in the knowledge of human beings: Andreas Binzer, that caricature of the domineering, egotistical male, begins to take on human form, frail though not villainous, as Stanley Burnell; the wife and the grandmother are no longer depressed drudges but the more plausible managers and diplomats of a middle-class home. Compared with her later work, the two stories are slighter and more mechanical, while the traits of self-idealization and self-pity (assuming that Kezia and Helen are childhood portraits of Katherine Mansfield) are far more prominent. The remaining stories of the volume (except 'Carnation' and two which were written after the publication in 1920 of *Bliss*) range through the Continent and the various strata of English suburbia, and call for little comment: they are usually entertaining, sometimes forced, and (to adapt the editor's curious note), few would have been reprinted had the author lived.

The next published work, *Prelude* (1918), in which Katherine Mansfield turned again to the scene of her childhood, shows an immense advance on anything previously attempted and the maturing of a technique now perfectly adapted to her needs. Behind this return are certain facts of biography that help to explain the special quality of her later stories. 'The war had come as a profound spiritual shock to her,' wrote her husband in the introduction to her *Journal* (1927), '. . . For a long period the chaos into which her thoughts and ideals and purposes had been flung remained unresolved. Then slowly her mind began to turn back towards her early childhood as a life which had existed apart from, and uncontaminated by, the mechanical civilization which had produced the war.'[12]

New Zealand, the idealized New Zealand of her childhood, became a refuge into which she withdrew from surroundings that, with sickness of mind and body, became more and more distasteful. With 'a kind of *possession*', an almost religious self-dedication that distinguishes her later New Zealand stories from those written before the war, she set about re-creating in minute detail the scenes and figures of her life in Wellington.[13] Perhaps only one of her contemporaries or a member of her family can appreciate fully the exactitude of her descriptions and the superb way in which she recalled a Wellington in the awkward stage of transition between small town and city. Its buildings, its social gatherings, its proverbial wind, its smells and sounds and personages, even its special brand of snobbery (coming oddly from the creator of Ma Parker) are evoked with a wonderful fidelity. Over all is cast the rose-coloured haze of nostalgic recollection. The settings are frequently described at dawn or dusk or bathed in moonlight, and pervading the stories is a certain languorous serenity, intensified by the leisurely movement of the descriptive passages. In keeping with the settings are the incidents—for plots, in the accepted sense, are rare. Most often these incidents belong to the world of children, where a night voyage, a seaside holiday, the removal of a household are portentous events. And when we examine it closely, the world of adults is little more complex or disturbing. The problems are never more serious than those of a tranquil household, the feelings rarely more intense than Beryl's vague discontent or Linda's recoil from her 'Newfoundland dog'. Even in 'The Garden Party', where tragedy intrudes, it is tragedy, intense but not very profound, as seen through the eyes of a young girl, bewildered by the 'diversity of life' and the effort to 'fit in every thing, Death included', as Katherine Mansfield herself explained.[14]

It was in handling this narrow range of experience during the last phase before her death in 1923 that Katherine Mansfield's genius finally flowered. In the dozen or so New Zealand stories of these years she wrought, as Arthur Sewell has said, 'a new texture out of English words', 'she communicated a quality of emotional experience found nowhere else in literature.'[15] She also realized the ambition, expressed in her *Journal*, of making her 'undiscovered country leap into the eyes of the Old World'.[16] Her compatriots are prone to regard this as the beginning and end of Katherine Mansfield's achievement, whereas, in fact, the fame she won for herself and her country is the least important and perhaps the least permanent part of her contribution. She is primarily important to New Zealanders because she interpreted accurately and beautifully a fragment of New Zealand life and a part of the New Zealand landscape. And to its writers she stands as an example of the self-dedication and the never-ending struggle towards personal integrity without which literature, in the highest sense, is impossible.

Some of the disadvantages of New Zealand's native hemisphere in this period may be illustrated from the writings of two women who worked in the same medium as Katherine Mansfield and who, at least in potentialities, were not immeasurably inferior to the author of *In a German Pension*. Alice F. Webb, the less sophisticated of the two, does not seem to have moved far beyond the confines of the rural and small-town life which she describes in a handful of sketches, *Miss Peter's Special* (1926), and while the limitations of such an environment are everywhere apparent they have supplied the conditions for the expression of a slender though admirable talent. The writer's materials are the scenes, manners, social recreations, personalities of a peaceful community, described with humour but without sentimentality. The writer herself is too deeply involved in that life to sentimentalize it, yet she is sufficiently 'emerged' to penetrate it accurately and sometimes profoundly. B. E. Baughan, the second of these two foils, is a writer of wider interests and experience, capable of commenting, 'Art comes at all times scantly to the back-blocks; and with what hope can Literature appeal to brains exhausted already by the exhaustion of the body? While, on the other hand, what have we in the place of these, to exercise our higher faculties, and so give us, in addition to material existence, *life*?'[17] This quotation from a book of rural sketches, *Brown Bread from a Colonial Oven* (1912), indicates both the writer's strength and her weakness. The collection lacks those unpremeditated qualities which have passed into Alice Webb's sketches, and there is a tendency to idyllize and to moralize rather than to interpret. But *Brown Bread* also shows, as does its author's verse, evidence of a mind unusually aware of significant themes and related technical problems. She experiments in 'Grandmother Speaks' with the colloquial soliloquy (a form later to be used more successfully by Frank Sargeson), she treats the situation of the *déraciné* with sympathetic understanding, and draws an interesting if slightly sentimental portrait of a 'civilized' Maori. But the book remains, like *Miss Peter's Special*, a series of exercises never followed up by more mature work; and this is the chief point of the comparison with Katherine Mansfield: that these two women, living and writing in New Zealand, were without the stimulus, the critical guidance, and the material advantages which assisted the callow apprentice of *In a German Pension* to transform herself into the author of *Prelude*. Along with many other first and last publications belonging to this period, these two books are evidence of the lack in New Zealand of all but the minimum conditions necessary for the creation of literature.

To persist as a writer in the face of discouragement or, worse, indifference required the unusual strength of character and tenacity of purpose shown by William Satchell, the only important novelist of the years immediately before 1914. In his best novel, *The Toll of the Bush* (1905), and to a smaller extent in *The Land of the Lost* (1902) Satchell reveals himself as an exceedingly minor Thomas Hardy, his Wessex the north of Auckland, his provincials the settlers and wanderers of that district, urged on by a destiny resembling Hardy's President of the Immortals, though less inexorably tragic in its dispensations. As the oracular Mrs. Gird in *The Toll of the Bush* affirms, ' "the order of things is not changed in deference to human desire. In the end we have to make up our minds to the inevitable." '[18] Like Hardy, Satchell was hampered by adherence to the conventions of nineteenth-century fiction, with its lining up of 'good' and 'bad' characters and its reliance on coincidence, undelivered letters, and similar expedients, while his extensive use of the remittance man points back to a type of New Zealand novel which seemed to have died out in the nineties.

Satchell's strength is not in his plots nor, for the most part, in his principal characters, but in his varied and authentically drawn minor figures and in his power of conveying the atmosphere of what is at once the most tropical and the most desolate part of the country. For perhaps the first time in New Zealand fiction a setting is not described as for an outside audience or smeared on in daubs of local colour, but subtly informs the book, influencing the nature of the characters and their actions. Pervading the novels is a sense of vast natural forces which lends dignity to the efforts of man and at the same time places them in perspective. It is one of Satchell's achievements that he suggests this background while he does justice to the complex and sometimes very commonplace human scene. The heroes and the villains are drawn much according to an established formula, but there are intermediate types, ranging from Andersen, the drunken weakling of *The Toll of the Bush*, to Hamilton, the mellow if occasionally irascible doctor in *The Land of the Lost*. In the interstices of both novels are packed many observations on life in the back-blocks, the product, like the minor characters, of a quick eye and a comprehending heart.

Though it is well constructed and dignified by an unusual theme, Satchell's third novel, *The Elixir of Life* (1907), suffers by contrast with its predecessors. The ocean was a poor substitute for the gum-fields, and the conduct of a shipload of New Zealanders gave the author only limited scope for his gift of sympathetic portraiture—it called rather for the humorist or the satirist. After an interval of seven years, there followed Satchell's best-known work, *The Greenstone Door* (1914), a carefully written historical novel set in the period between the eighteen-thirties and the close of the Maori wars. Satchell had obviously gone to great pains to reconstruct the life of this vanished era, and both his descriptions of ancient Maori customs and his portraits of historical figures (including one, highly idealized, of Sir George Grey) can be read with interest and some profit. As a novel, however, the book fails: too much is described and explained, not enough presented through the interplay of characters and the development of action; the characters themselves are too wooden to carry much conviction, the plot is more improbable and melodramatic than ever, and the Maoris do not rise far above the level of those in the novels of Wilson and White. Satchell is not successful in the presentation of Maoris even in his earlier work, where they are usually introduced to provide humorous relief (a substitute for Hardy's comic peasants).

Indeed, the only imaginative writer of this period who did anything like justice to the Maoris was William Baucke. In a collection of sketches, *Where the White Man Treads* (1905), he sets down in rapid, exuberant prose animated portraits of Maoris met casually on expeditions, legends gathered at the hearth-side, debates, gossip, penetrating character studies, comparisons between the old Maori and his degenerate successor. To all this he adds his own incisive commentary, settling moral issues with all the expedition and finality of the back-blocks philosopher. Elsewhere in essays and fiction, with only rare exceptions, the Maori emerged in crude outline as an inferior version of Fenimore Cooper's Red Indian or as a peg on which to hang some mildly salacious sermon on the half-caste problem. New Zealand society at this time was unable to focus itself; much less could it define and express its attitude towards a native race; and outside the work of anthropologists and the records of the Polynesian Society it was usually the fate of the Maoris to be exploited or sentimentalized.

Satchell's work came to an abrupt close in 1914, but in the early post-war years the north of Auckland again formed the scene of a group of novels by a writer of some distinction, Jane Mander. *The Story of a New Zealand River* (1920) and its successors are not so much a continuation of Satchell's early work as a treatment of the same life on gum-fields and in timber settlements from a feminine point of view which brought with it interests and preoccupations linking Jane Mander with Edith Searle Grossmann and, more tenuously, with Katherine Mansfield. Her first novel (probably, as the title suggests, written in the shadow of Olive Schreiner's *Story of an African Farm*), has as its principal theme the gradual transformation of an Englishwoman who marries a colonial and makes her home in an isolated settlement of the Kaipara district. The delicately nurtured Alice Roland (who, as her daughter Asia remarks, ' "loves everything that comes from England" ') is ill equipped for such a life, and her situation is not improved by the complete lack of sympathy between herself and her able but uncouth husband, 'the boss' (a rural and cruder Stanley Burnell).[19] She finds relief and guidance from three sources: from her neighbour Mrs. Brayton, who has established a corner of England in the wilds of Kaipara; more dangerously from her husband's foreman, an English remittance man doctor; and from Asia, who represents the emancipated generation brought up in colonial surroundings with the additional advantage of George Bernard Shaw's teachings. Finally, a solution and a happy ending are found (rather crassly) in the boss's heroic death.

The chief defects of the book are an excessive emotionalism, which sometimes brings it down to the level of a novelette, and the occasional falsity of the plot. Superior in these respects is *Allen Adair* (1925) in which the situation is more convincing because it is more banal and at the same time more serious. The central figure of this novel is the son of middle-class parents who, thinking to establish him in life, determine, in spite of his opposition, to send him to Oxford: 'A son at Oxford. Quite exciting. And they were much annoyed when Allen shrank from the prospect. . . . Not want to go to Oxford!'[20] The Oxford experiment fails, and Allen finds himself only when he returns to New Zealand and, to his family's chagrin, settles down as a storekeeper on the gum-fields. The struggle between middle-class ambitions and his own desire for a life of placid mediocrity reaches a more acute stage when his city-born wife, a devoted mother and efficient housekeeper, but vain and thoroughly material in her outlook, urges him to return to the city. There is no 'happy ending' to this book which closes on the more plausible note of stalemate and partial compromise.

Besides the interest they have in their exploration of human problems in the years centred on the First World War Jane Mander's novels have what may be termed a documentary value. Each one is built up round some occupation or industry: the scene of *The New Zealand River* is a timber-milling settlement; the heroine of *The Passionate Puritan* (1922) is a country schoolteacher; small-town journalism and politics form the background of *The Strange Attraction* (1923), storekeeping and gum-digging of *Allen Adair*. In thus bringing New Zealand fiction into closer touch with the social environment, she not only made an original contribution but also cleared the way for several writers of the nineteen-thirties. Credit is also due to her for introducing a freer and healthier tone into New Zealand letters. As Jean Devanny was to do in a more lurid way, Jane Mander broke many of the taboos which had been too studiously observed by New Zealand writers, though not by New Zealand society. For her temerity she was the target of hostile criticism which, it is said, ended her career as a novelist. This was the more regrettable because in all four of her New Zealand novels, especially in the first and last, there are clear signs of that 'something fresh and sturdy' which, in the course of a somewhat grudging review, Katherine Mansfield discerned 'under all the false wrappings' of *The New Zealand River*.[21]

To discard the 'wrappings' of conventional English fiction—the contrivances of plot, the literary language, the banalities of thought and utterance—called for the combination of art and self-knowledge to which Katherine Mansfield herself attained; or, on the other hand, it required the innocent integrity of Frank S. Anthony. In a series of sketches, later collected under the title of *Me and Gus* (1938), this young naval veteran turned dairy farmer all unknowingly (one suspects) effected during the early twenties a minor revolution in New Zealand fiction. Avoiding the bleached diction used by most of his predecessors, he drew on the vernacular of his time and calling to depict, in humorous terms, his experiences on a derelict Taranaki farm. The broad masculine humour of the sketches, their unfailing gusto, and their wholesome bucolic flavour had been absent from New Zealand writing since pioneer days. Indeed, it was a belated outpost of pioneering that Anthony expressed—a community dominantly male, delighting in practical joke and horse-play, sardonic and self-depreciatory, warring with the 'women folk' whom at the same time it idealized. Even more original (for in composing the sketches Anthony had American and Australian examples to guide him) was a novel, *Follow the Call* (1936). Here, against the same background of rural and small-town life, he told the story of a *grande passion*. The style is more subdued than that of the sketches, but, with its nervous colloquial directness, it succeeds in creating a wholly convincing picture of the cockatoo hero, his surroundings, and his tragi-comic infatuation. Nowhere else in New Zealand writing have the thoughts and feelings of the ordinary 'joker' been explored with such compassionate insight. The career, so promisingly begun, came to an untimely end. Even Anthony, it seems, could not resist the prevailing current of his times: he left New Zealand, his biographer relates, 'to try his fortune in London.'[22] There, his health undermined by war injuries, he died early in 1925. During his lifetime and for more than a decade afterwards his work met with little recognition. In the more favourable climate of the thirties, the novel found a publisher. The sketches were later collected and have since been subjected to the sad indignity of 'revision and rewriting' to meet the tastes of a 'wider audience'.[23]

Again, as so often in this period, the stress falls on the limitations of the New Zealand environment. But while imaginative writers were meeting with indifference or hostile criticism, a distinctive literature, the work of native-born writers and chiefly historical and anthropological in substance, was assuming impressive proportions. In the nineties, it has already been seen, there was evidence of a growing interest in the country's past, stimulated, in some degree, by national and provincial jubilees. A further incentive was the realization that both Maoris and Europeans of the older generations were dying out and with them oral records of the past. The foundation of a local scholarship owed little to the University of New Zealand, but was due chiefly to the efforts of disinterested men, usually self-trained and often hampered by lack of means and the most elementary facilities for research. It is a scholarship which inevitably reflects these circumstances: it sometimes leans too heavily on the oral reminiscence and may, on occasion, exasperate through its blithe disregard of source and reference; on the other hand, it has the colour and concreteness gained from direct contact with the repositories of history, while it shows the zest of work undertaken not for gain nor as academic labour but from deep-rooted, even passionate, interest in the past. It is impossible to review here the voluminous writings of S. Percy Smith, Elsdon Best, T. Lindsay Buick, and their associates and successors, but the interests of this group, together with scientific interests of much earlier origin, were to unite in one work of the period. *Tutira* (1921) was entitled 'The Story of a New Zealand Sheep Station'; such is the originality of its conception, such the breadth of its implications, that it forms in little 'The Story of New Zealand'.

In the light of theorizings about a 'native' culture, it is a little curious to reflect on the circumstances in which this distinctively New Zealand work made its appearance. Contrary to the assumptions of prophets in the nineties, *Tutira* owed nothing to a deliberately national movement; its author worked almost in isolation, and although he was clearly not independent of contemporary influences, they reached him, as it were, 'subcutaneously.' Nor was *Tutira* an 'imaginative' work, enriched though it is by qualities which both poets and novelists might well envy. Finally, its author was not, in the strictest sense, a New Zealander—thus, perhaps, escaping the worst effects of a 'mother fixation' which seemed to assume its most virulent form in the native New Zealander. H. Guthrie-Smith was born in Scotland, received his formal education at Rugby, and came to New Zealand in the early eighties. After gaining some experience as a cadet in Canterbury, he took up an abandoned sheep run in northern Hawke's Bay. This run, Tutira, remained his home for the rest of his long life and formed the subject of his first and greatest book.

As originally planned, *Tutira* was to have described only the natural history of the run. Later, to the good fortune of his readers, Guthrie-Smith extended its scope to include 'chapters on physiography, native life, pioneer work, and surface alterations'. The book thus goes far beyond White's *Natural History of Selborne* to trace the story of a fragment of New Zealand from the hypothetic era of its immersion in the sea until the time when it was occupied and precariously subdued by Europeans. Most of the account is taken up with that relatively brief moment of time since the arrival of man, but the early chapters, with their description of the geology, physical features, climate, and general configuration of the Tutira area, are interesting in themselves and intimately connected with what follows. As the author remarks of two intimidating pages of tabulated returns, 'These details of rainfall have been given not merely as meteorological data of an impersonal sort; the climate of Tutira has deeply affected the fortunes of the station. . . . Excessive rainfall has been the bane of the place, retarding its development by years.' To which is attached one of Guthrie-Smith's characteristic footnotes, compressing into a couple of sentences the whole ethos of the farming community: 'One observer whose case I recall was requested by neighbours to cease to forward his returns. "Science may be right enough, perhaps, in its proper place," they declared, "but he was ruining the district and hampering settlement with his blessed rainfalls." '[24]

The Maori section, corresponding to White's 'Antiquities', reconstructs the period of native occupation with the patience, the assiduous attention to detail, and the comprehending imagination that pervade the book. Though he would have claimed to be no more than amateur anthropologist, Guthrie-Smith made useful contributions both to anthropological technique and, in a smaller way, to Maori lore. His narrowly local method was the perfect one for the study of a people who, in their primitive state, were not a nation but a number of tribes and sub-tribes confined, for the most part, to limited areas. No other writer, except Elsdon Best, brings out so well and so concretely the organic nature of Maori culture—the close connexion between locality, occupation, climate on the one hand and tradition, poem, and folk-tale on the other.

When, after formidable chapters on the native covering and

avifauna of the station, man enters for the second time, the longest and most interesting part of the book begins, an account of the acclimatization of Europeans on Tutira—European man and the birds, animals, insects, plants that followed in his wake or preceded him. Man, the author explains in his preface, is to be treated as 'a beast of the field': 'The early failure of *homo sapiens* on Tutira, his ultimate acclimatization, has been noted, as far as may be, in terms of the weasel or rabbit. . . .' The qualification is necessary, for the adaptation of man proves to be a long and complex process; it involves the acquisition of business experience, the ability to handle a tribe of Maori landlords, and sufficient shrewdness to circumvent sinister loan-sharks in the town near by; more important still, it means acquiring an intimate knowledge of the run—its soil, its climate, its bearing capacity, its suitability for this or that breed of sheep. Guthrie-Smith comments on the defeat of his predecessors, 'The truth is, that from the beginning these pioneers were doomed—they were predestined—to failure. Conditions in the interior were in those days quite unknown; knowledge of local conditions—the most important knowledge of all—had to be purchased.'[25]

In his descriptions of the native bush, the author has already shown himself to be something of a poet. Signs of the latent novelist now appear. Despite the professed aim of studying *homo sapiens* in terms of the weasel or the rabbit, the story of early failures and ultimate success on Tutira is told with humour, understanding, and imagination. For example, Guthrie-Smith sees behind the rough jottings of a farm diary a picture of 'smoky huts lit by candles guttering in the draughts, the writer, with hard hands and broken nails, rising from time to time to turn the frizzling chops, to prong the simmering joint, or to pile fresh embers on the lid of the camp oven'. The same power of discerning the manifold associations which surround an object is again seen when Guthrie-Smith turns to consider the aliens of Tutira, the plants and animals brought to the station deliberately or by chance. A clump of mint on the site of a deserted *pa*, an aged grove of peaches, a patch of ryegrass—these and other 'children of the church' are traced back (here with the addition of an anecdote, there with a vividly described scene) to the Bay of Islands, whence they were dispersed by missionaries, neophytes, and scholars. The progress of the blackberry, 'that fatal and perfidious plant,' is reconstructed as a master detective might some ramifying conspiracy.[26] So, with the method and the emotion appropriate to each, Guthrie-Smith treats the many aliens with which man in his wisdom and his ignorance has populated a hitherto virgin tract.

When European settlement of New Zealand was beginning on a large scale, Dieffenbach had reflected, 'What a chain of alterations . . . takes place from the introduction by man of a single animal into a country where it was before unknown!' By a fortunate chance, a later colonist was superbly equipped to observe and record this basic phenomenon—basic because it is, in essence, the phenomenon of colonization itself. For some forty years Guthrie-Smith noted the results of each fresh impact on his chosen area and the gradual, never-completed process of adaptation which followed. As he well knew, it was a process to which man was subject no less than the rest of nature, and Guthrie-Smith no less than other men. Not the least interesting theme of *Tutira* is the transformation of the young Scot who took up land hoping it would 'provide after a few seasons easy enlargement of . . . minds and fortunes, endless rivers, moors, and forests in Scotland'. The change of outlook is made explicit in Guthrie-Smith's tribute to 'his dear adopted land'; it is implicit in the whole book.[27] The exile had become a New Zealander—a New Zealander in accord, as few have been, with his country in all its diversity of land and water, plant life and animal life, nature and man.

In the course of time, Tutira did provide some enlargement of fortune, part of which Guthrie-Smith devoted to a more extensive study of nature (particularly bird life) than was possible within the confines of Tutira. The results of these excursions to many districts of New Zealand and to some of its outlying islands were published in a series of books which closed in 1936 with *Sorrows and Joys of a New Zealand Naturalist*. Though they cannot compare with *Tutira* in range of subject or originality of conception, these pleasantly discursive volumes add not only to the knowledge of New Zealand nature but to the portrait of Guthrie-Smith.

Increasingly with the years he indulged a reflective bent—part serious, part dryly humorous—already manifest in *Tutira*, but more fully expressed in the masterly opening chapters of *Sorrows and Joys*. There he looked back, as a naturalist, on the history of New Zealand from the time when, in 'the landing of Cook, nay in the momentary glimpse by Tasman of that "large high lieing land"', came 'the seeds of death' to this country. Reproaching himself for his share in the 'ravishment of the Dominion', he concluded, 'Only that it is impossible for any individual to withstand the stream of tendency, to divaricate from lines aeons ago laid down must be the writer's partial exoneration.'[28] Thus Guthrie-Smith called the shades of determinism to his aid. Seeking some further atonement for its crimes, European civilization in New Zealand might point to a few of its finer products, among them the works of H. Guthrie-Smith.

The cleavage in New Zealand's imaginative life at this time reveals itself even more profoundly in poetry than in prose. Few poets found themselves in a position to embark on the voyage 'Home', still fewer emigrated permanently, but all—or nearly all—were in one degree or another spiritual exiles. Not infrequently they indulged in nostalgic dreams of the old world. They found it more natural to use the traditional language of English poets than the very different idiom of their own country. The swallow and the nightingale came to their minds almost as readily as the fantail and the tui—and the tui was sometimes no more than a nightingale in New Zealand garb. Physically they remained in their own country; as poets they dwelt twelve thousand miles away.

Reasons for the poetic *malaise* of the nineteen-hundreds and nineteen-twenties are not far to seek. As the most delicately constituted members of the community, poets were more sensitive than others to the dominant emotion of their time, an emotion that was strengthened by their almost complete dependence on English literature. For the dangers inherent in New Zealand's colonial status were most noticeable in the very period when the country became a Dominion and acquired an indeterminate measure of nationhood. That the Bowens and the Dometts should read and write as Englishmen was natural, indeed inevitable; though they had set up homes at the antipodes, they were, after all, still Englishmen. For New Zealanders, sometimes of the second colonial generation, to visit in their literary excursions solely a region of scenes, images, and ideas not merely foreign to them but, in some respects, contrary to the facts of their experience—this was different and more dangerous. The most serious consequence was not, however, the occasional confusion of seasons in the minds of young readers but the creation of an abstract, idealized, often sentimentalized 'literary' world, remote from both poles of reality, the English writer's and the colonial reader's. This was the imaginative world of all but a few of New Zealand's versifiers and poets in the years under review.

It was symptomatic of the times that poetry tended, after the nineties, to become increasingly 'private'. The work of Jessie Mackay and Pember Reeves had its limitations, but much of it did at least spring from interests shared by most New Zealanders. Their successors, quite comprehensibly, found little to inspire them in the spectacle of increasing prosperity. So they turned either to the trite exaltation of natural beauty or inward to the commemoration of feelings which, in the absence of literary distinction, could move the reader only to boredom or a mild embarrassment. Thus New Zealand poetry retired into the isolation it had known in the years of pioneering. But the robust self-assurance of Domett and his fellow-writers had vanished. The poetic flood now dried up to a thin trickle of lyric verse, sonnets, triolets, indicative of a final stage in the exhaustion of the romantic tradition. When an external influence made itself felt, it was in the pre-1914 years the degenerate classicism of *Bulletin* Bohemians and later the work of Rupert Brooke, not without its interest in expressing the lush, eager lyricism of the Georgian movement, but wholly disastrous to its colonial imitators.

This view of the poetic landscape is true only of its broad outlines: apt turns of phrase, flashes of wit and imagination, a few wholly satisfying poems modify the picture of unrelieved mediocrity. And even in the first decade of the century, notably in two collections by B. E. Baughan, there are signs of fresh life and experiment. The use in *Reuben* (1903) of a colloquial ballad form, borrowed from Australia, showed a desire to break with the prevailing conventions, and in *Shingle Short* (1908) the same writer came to grips with local material in several interesting experiments. The title poem is a lengthy rhymed monologue, written in a hybrid dialect of New Zealand rural slang and literary Australianese, which is placed in the mouth of a half-wit:

> *Thank God for this ungodly rain!*
> *Paddock's a puddle, creek's in flood,*
> *Road's like a river mix'd up rich—*
> *Pea-soup, treacle, pudd'n an' sich—*
> *Reggular marmalade o' mud.*
> *Won't be no larrikins to-night,*
> *Come peerin', jeerin' thro' the pane!*[29]

It is obvious that this is too deliberately colloquial, too consciously masculine; moreover, sustained as it is through some thirty pages and combined with pseudo-philosophical trimmings, it becomes monotonous in the extreme. Nevertheless, the poem is of great interest as an early attempt at stylization in terms of New Zealand idiom and domestic imagery. The same originality is shown in several other poems of the collection, and even where the form is traditional a shoot of new life may be seen breaking through the old integument. Something similar might be said of Whitman's early work, and Whitmanesque (though not derivatively so) is the closing invocation of 'Maui's Fish':

> *Alive! Yea, Te Ika—*
> *Of the Bone of the Past, of the Blood of the Present,*
> *Here, at the end of the earth, in the first of the Future,*
> *Thou standest, courageous and youthful, a country to come!*[30]

This frontal attack on the special problems of New Zealand verse cannot be paralleled among native New Zealanders—for B. E. Baughan, like Guthrie-Smith, had the advantages of birth and education in Britain. England to her was a reality, not a dominating abstraction, and her boldness contrasts with the initial conservatism of the two New Zealand-born successors of Reeves and Jessie Mackay.

The affinity between Reeves and Alan Mulgan is shown in their strikingly similar 'Passing of the Forest' and 'Dead Timber', more indirectly in the younger writer's handling of genuinely apprehended local themes. 'Soldier Settlement,' for example, is inspired by a social conscience more common in the nineties than in the easy-going years that followed:

> *Haggard he looks about his world—*
> *The leaning shack, the broken fence,*
> *The little flag of green unfurled*
> *Before the forest's walled defence....*[31]

The content of these verses, like that of *Golden Wedding* (1932), a descriptive poem in rhymed couplets, is indigenous enough, but in both cases one feels that the form is not well chosen and, furthermore, not thoroughly acclimatized. Such lines as these from *Golden Wedding* remind the reader too insistently of illustrious precedent:

> *In rusty black the ageing vicar smiles,*
> *Priest of a flock that straggles thirty miles.*
>   . . . . .
> *Stifling regret, outfacing household fear,*
> *Six mouths, two hundred doubtful pounds a year.*[32]

Drawn with greater originality is the affectionate picture of the aged couple, gathered to receive the felicitations of their clan, or the shrewd portrait of the local member of Parliament. Altogether, the poem displays virtues rare enough in New Zealand at this period—a mild humour, a warm domestic sentiment, an intimate knowledge of rural manners and modes of expression. But here, as in the writer's earlier verse, the monotonous rhythm and sometimes feeble rhymes indicate a slack conception of the poetic craft, while the strong imitative element suggests an overpowering sense of the prestige of English literature.

Eileen Duggan, the poetic heir of Jessie Mackay, was the most promising talent to appear in the years immediately after the

First World War. Depending on a fitful and uncertain impulse, she has throughout her long career been far from prolific: at the outset, in *Poems* (1921) she wrote, 'Song comes to me / But haltingly. . . .'[33] The sensitive young poet revealed in this collection possessed a good deal in common with Jessie Mackay—a hatred of tyranny, sympathy with the weak or the oppressed, and a devout Catholicism which replaced the older poet's diffused humanitarianism. The output of the next two decades was contained in three small books, the first of which, *New Zealand Bird Songs* (1929), was written for children and did not, the poet modestly emphasized, 'pretend to be literature.'[34] As compared with the earliest volume, *Poems* (1937) showed some loss of vigour but also a more than compensating refinement in language and sensibility. The collection was notable for felicitous lines and phrases, as:

> *Lost in a great green jeopardy of sea. . . .*

or
> *her body's blame*
> *Burnt in a crucible of shame. . . .*

or
> *Running in little circles like a foal*
> *Around a dying and defiant mother.*[35]

Less often was a complete poem carried through at this level, and the forced or inappropriate conceit was almost as common as the apt image: in the last quotation, for example, it is the moon that is 'running in little circles'! Some of the most successful poems, unified by a mood of retrospection, had their setting in childhood and a vividly remembered countryside. Perhaps the best is the oft-quoted, justly admired 'Twilight'.

Eileen Duggan has gone farther than any other poet of recent times in drawing on Maori words and traditions and the material of New Zealand history. This element of her work is most fully developed in *New Zealand Poems* (1940) which opened with a 'Centenary Ode', essaying the difficult task of celebrating the nation's history from its beginnings in the mythical age of Kupe. There is scholarship in the ode and a profound feeling for New Zealand (more especially the Cook Strait area); but the writer is no more capable than her predecessors were of animating the ancient myths and fusing the two cultures. Less ambitious is 'The Charting', a distinguished achievement in the intractable *genre* of poeticized history. Eileen Duggan's patriotism, it would seem, is intense but narrow (to adapt Mrs. Grossmann); it finds its happiest expression in her Marlborough poems and in an associated group, somewhat 'folksy' but authentic—among them 'The Bushwoman', 'The Drayman', 'The Blacksmith's Wife'— which commemorate rustic virtues and the manners of a past age.

The next work, *More Poems* (1951), shows a marked change in mood and technique, a change whose nature may be suggested by brief quotations from three poems:

*now she goes
Into life's awful wisdom at its close,
Alive at last and naked of conceits.*

Poets are point-blank and dire. . . .

Have done with words that are no more than sounds![36]

There are few 'memorable' single lines in this collection, isolated conceits are rare, and many of the earlier themes have vanished. In the decade since *New Zealand Poems* a new poet has emerged, spare of utterance, sometimes vehement, always disciplined, her affinities now lying rather with the metaphysicals than with the romantics. In taut, gnomic verse and lean lyric she broods on or debates the 'awful wisdom' of 'our dreadful days'.[37] Her subject is often war, occasionally treated with a faint gesture of conventional patriotism (as in 'Greece'), more often viewed with a grief and a compassion that transcend both nationality and faction. Her explicitly religious poems, which in earlier collections were devout, decorative, fanciful, but rarely deep, acquire urgency and power as the poet extends the limits of faith to embrace her sombre wisdom. It is a remarkable achievement, the transformation in late maturity of long-established poetic habits in response to the pressure of inner experience. *More Poems*—and its successors —will stand as the consummation and crown of Eileen Duggan's austere pursuit of the poetic vocation.

VII
The Thirties

THE growth of culture in a new soil is unpredictable; it follows no established sequence, is subject to no universal law. All one can assert with certainty is that it requires time for germination and the indispensable seeds of talent. Thus at the close of the nineteen-twenties there was no obvious sign that the years ahead were to be the most fertile in New Zealand's literary history. True, the country was within sight of its first centenary; but the cultural process is not susceptible to the magic of numbers, nor indeed is one hundred years a large unit in the measure of civilization. The requisite talent was present, as we now realize; for the most part, however, it had revealed itself as yet only in obscure places or lay dormant, awaiting the necessary conditions for growth. The nature of these conditions, again, cannot be simply or certainly stated. It is perhaps enough to say that the most fruitful literary decade of New Zealand's first century began with a depression and ended with a war. In a few agitated years a handful of men and women produced a body of work which, in an intimate and organic sense, belonged to the country as none of its previous writings had done. They created the nucleus of a literature where there had existed before only isolated achievement.

One of the first clear hints of a new literary impulse was the publication early in 1932 of *Phoenix* by a group of Auckland students and their sympathizers. In its earliest incarnation and under its first editor, James Bertram, *Phoenix* was 'primarily a literary magazine', its 'background . . . literary; its policy aesthetic'.[1] It derived its title from D. H. Lawrence, modelled itself on John Middleton Murry's *New Adelphi*, quoted T. S. Eliot, and ministered to the cult of Katherine Mansfield. With the deepening of the depression and the appointment of R. A. K.

Mason as editor, the periodical changed both format and character. Now aggressively 'modern' in appearance, it transferred its allegiance from Murry to Marx and used a larger proportion of its space to discuss political and economic issues, international as well as local.

Not since the nineties had there been such healthy evidence of intellectual and spiritual unrest among New Zealand youth. And, speaking generally, the writers of *Phoenix* compared more than favourably with their predecessors of the earlier generation: they were more confident, far more critical, better informed and better educated. Their confidence, it is true, sometimes took form in an insufferable omniscience, and they were prone to the pontifical ponderings and solemn evaluations which are so often the marks of youthful enterprise. But implicit in the undertaking was a conviction that things of the mind and spirit were worth considering, worth writing about, indeed worth suffering for. *Phoenix* was a challenge to New Zealand complacency and to the dominance of material standards. More than that, it was a challenge to the attitude of timid provincialism which had characterized New Zealand writing in the earlier years of the century. 'Are we poor that we should beg or steal?' asked one contributor, at the same time supplying an answer, 'let us work with our hands and the sweat of our low brows until we have our own wealth to scatter.' Even London, now associated with economic thraldom, had lost some of its old glamour: 'Let us in New Zealand not lament too much that we are away from the centre of things, from the squabbles and bickerings and literary cabals.'[2] So urged two critics of the first number with its (in their opinion) excessive reliance on the Adelphic oracle.

Only four numbers of *Phoenix* were published, and, except for a handful of poems, its contents were ephemeral in nature. Nevertheless, as a symptom and a beginning, it has an important place in the history of the thirties. It illustrates that combination of ideals, aesthetic and political, which was to invigorate—and sometimes bedevil—the entire decade. It encouraged a spirit of disciplined experiment among the young. It formed a rallying-point for those who had little hope of publication elsewhere. It did something to establish Auckland as the chief centre of New Zealand writing. Finally, and not least important, it revealed an interest in typography rare in New Zealand up to that time. That *Phoenix* was no mere flash in the pan is proved by what happened in the years that followed. Its views on the need for a fresh orientation in New Zealand letters were taken up and developed, explicitly in an essay by A. R. D. Fairburn, which might be taken as the unofficial manifesto of the group, by implication in the work of the writers themselves. For, when *Phoenix* perished, most of its circle found other means of self-expression. Some became regular contributors to the Christchurch journal *Tomorrow*, first published in 1934. Some wrote occasionally for the quarterly *Art in New Zealand* which had been founded in 1928 and, despite great difficulties, continued publication throughout the lean depression years. To these resources were added those of the presses which R. W. Lowry, typographer of *Phoenix*, conjured from its ashes and the Caxton Press of Christchurch, founded by Denis Glover. These presses, the Caxton more especially, played a vital part in the thirties (as they have in later years). Besides the function they served in bringing out work beyond the range of established publishers, they were largely instrumental in raising New Zealand's deplorably low standards of book-production. In this decade it became possible to produce local books whose format was no longer a reproach to their country of origin, and though a London imprint still retained many advantages, one of the barriers to publication—and therefore to writing—was removed. It was owing to the existence of these presses (and also to reasons more fundamental and more difficult to explain) that its two most widely divergent cities became New Zealand's cultural centres. Auckland, with its larger, more cosmopolitan population, its freedom from strong traditional shackles, and its closer touch with America, maintained the leadership it had assumed with the publication of *Phoenix*. The junior partner was Christchurch, still retaining in its isolation a hold on the ideals implanted there by the Canterbury pilgrims.

To begin with, the movement took poetic form, first achieving mature expression in the work of two Aucklanders, A. R. D. Fairburn and R. A. K. Mason. Fairburn, the senior by a year or so, was a New Zealander of the fourth generation (as he proudly affirmed), who had returned from England after publishing there his first collection, *He Shall Not Rise* (1930). In the perspective supplied by the poet's later achievement, this book makes curious reading. The poems, a note explains, had been written in New Zealand—a fact that is obvious only in the occasional use of native names or in the theme of verses motivated by a kind of myth hunger. In one of these the poet fancies that Odysseus, voyaging in old age, set foot on New Zealand. A related idea inspires the brief 'In the Younger Land', perhaps the best poem in the collection. For the rest, the verses express a pagan but generally decorous delight in nature and the physical senses, a gentle, melancholy lyricism, and some slight facility in turning epigrams. Traces of T. S. Eliot are present, but in general the verse is Georgian, employing such vague poetic counters as 'silver forests', 'deep meadows', 'woodland streams' (all culled from one poem).[3] There is none of the later poet's concreteness, none of his wit, none of his intellectual curiosity, none of his energy. Only on its last page does there appear a clue to the understanding of the collection. The final poem, from which the book draws its title, begins:

Tonight I have taken all that I was
and strangled him that pale lily-white lad....[4]

He Shall Not Rise is an overt act of rejection, publicly proclaiming the burial of a dead poetic self.

A few years later the implications of that act were set out in the essay, already mentioned, in which Fairburn considered the situation of the New Zealand writer, traditionless, nostalgic for 'Home', 'Englishmen, born in exile'. That era of dependence, he said, was drawing to a close; in future writers must allow themselves to be 'influenced, but not enslaved' by the mother country. Moreover, to counterbalance the inevitable, unavoidable English influence, they might look elsewhere—the novelists, for instance, to the native American tradition running from Mark Twain to Ernest Hemingway. 'I believe,' he wrote, 'that from the point of view of the New Zealand writer, "Huckleberry Finn" is the most important novel ever written. . . . We can understand Huck, the true colonial, where we can only pretend to understand Tom Brown, the English public-school boy.' As for the poet, he must discard imitative fashions like the 'shoddy paganism' of Australian verse; he must discard Georgianism; he must discard the cosmopolitan and rootless view of art 'which claims of such-and-such a poem that it "might have been written anywhere".' The young New Zealand writer, he urged in memorable words, 'must be willing to partake, internally as well as externally, of the anarchy of life in a new place and, by his creative energy, give that life form and consciousness.'[5] For the next twenty years Fairburn addressed himself to the task he had so finely formulated. His creative powers, expended with boundless generosity, flowed in numerous directions, not all of them literary, not all of them profitable. But never, in the course of a crowded life, was he deflected from his true vocation—he never ceased to be a poet.

Until a definitive collection appears, Fairburn's poetic reputation will rest on two works, *Strange Rendezvous* and *Three Poems*, both published in 1952. The former includes shorter poems written from 1929 onwards and may thus be taken to represent the new phase which began after the appearance of *He Shall Not Rise*. The change is indeed remarkable, though the 'lily-white lad', it happily proves, was not wholly suppressed. He rises again, mature, invigorated, as the lyric impulse which runs through all Fairburn's poetry, a unifying element in its diversity. There are few explicit references to New Zealand in *Strange Rendezvous*. The cliffs, the sea, the caves, the trees are there, but only as a setting for the personal and human experience with which the poet is principally concerned. His two chief themes were already present in the first collection: 'the instant of love;/and the flat calm of death.'[6] Love now appears in all its complexity—love carnal, love spiritual, youthful love, wild love, or in 'Empty House', love domesticated:

> But when you come back, dead wood shall bud,
> warm and human this house shall be,

> brick will be brighter, bed more soft,
> there will be smells of fur and food
> and the scent of children's bodies.[7]

Sensuous, passionate, profound, these love poems are unique in our literature. Death, equally pervasive and equally protean, is refuge, foe, the source of honour, the gate to a qualified immortality. In the satirical poems, for which there is little precedent in the first collection, the targets are the rich, the worldly, the successful, or those who hold 'life synonymous with knowledge'.[8] The earlier verses of this kind are written with a gay exuberance that robs them of half their sting; in those added after 1941 a sourer note is sometimes audible, expressing a mood, it would seem, rather than a settled conviction. The impression left by *Strange Rendezvous* is of a poetic journal in which is recorded with eloquent honesty the varied response of an alert and sensitive mind to the flux of experience.

Three Poems, which includes Fairburn's longer works, bears a closer resemblance to *Strange Rendezvous* than would appear at first sight. The contents of the volume—or, at least, the two earlier works, *Dominion* and *The Voyage*—are not so much closely articulated long poems as groups of short poems and lyrics, differing in subject, mood, and form, but related to a central theme. *Dominion* opens with a picture of New Zealand during the depression. The poet surveys this crumbling society—its financial system, the church, the press, the institution of marriage—in an ecstasy of denunciation that tends to defeat his purpose: the brilliance and extravagance of his rhetoric distract attention from the evils he seeks to expose. The denunciation ends, and in a quieter mood, contemplative, reverent, retrospective, he turns to nature in whose resources he seems to discern some hope of man's renewal. The section gives way to one of disputation, and the poem then moves to its apocalyptic close. *The Voyage* is a less portentous work, often exploding in verbal pyrotechnics and occasionally verging towards the literary larrikinism that is given freer rein in *The Rakehelly Man* (1945). In intention, however, it is deeply serious, a poem (as Fairburn himself described it) 'about faith, and works', in which the nautical figures and properties take on universal meaning:

>   *Who are we*
> *to know the complete, illimitable pattern?*
> *Each to his business, tending ropes and gear,*
> *navigating or cooking, keeping log,*
> *fulfilling in each act our sacrament*
> *and simple story.*[9]

To a Friend in the Wilderness, the last poem of the sequence, approaches the problems of faith and works and being with greater directness. As if in a final testament, discarding the devices of allegory and symbol, Fairburn recorded in this poem his mature reflections on the material of his earlier work. The supple verse, beautifully controlled, flows on in argument and soliloquy, gathering up the familiar themes—love, death, nature, the 'mortal predicament'—until, in a splendid affirmation, the poet declares his humanistic faith:

> *These are my people. Till seventy times seven*
> *I am committed to them,*
> *which is neither a matter for pride nor a cause for grief:*
> *does the shaken leaf*
> *lay claim to the earth, or condemn*
> *the wind that blows out of heaven?*[10]

Of no poem can it be said more truly that it gives form and consciousness to the anarchy of life in New Zealand.

To turn from Fairburn to Mason is to pass from the disorder of a crowded living-room, warm and fruitful, to the cold austerity of a cell. The contrast between these two contemporaries, linked though they were by a common birthplace, by ties of friendship, and by a common vocation, is nowhere more evident than in their poetic beginnings. The earliest of Mason's verse (at least the small selection which can be readily consulted) shows few signs of the literary adolescence that was prolonged with Fairburn into the middle twenties. At the age of eighteen

Mason was an accomplished poet; before he was twenty he had published some of his best verse. The three poems he has considered worth salvaging from his first collection already hint at the manner and content of his mature work. The stripped language and tense rhythms, the fondness for strict forms (especially the sonnet), the macabre imagination and sombre intensity of feeling—these are present at the outset. In *The Beggar* (1924) the impression of startling precocity, though it persists, is modified by the inclusion of inferior material. The title poem, for example, is patently manufactured—a shallow idea decked out with worn and betraying phrases: 'fine old trees' feet', 'adown this lovely dale', 'Fields where frail pools sleeping are'.[11] Such lapses into the spuriously poetic are rare, but the pitch of the whole collection is somewhat lower than elsewhere in Mason's work. The poems are the self-communings of a troubled and solitary spirit rather than the protests of an agonized soul. The themes are life's evanescence, the inevitability of death, the loneliness of the individual. The figures of legend and history are more real to the young poet than his fellow-mortals: he sees Gaius Marius 'by Waitemata's tide', he domiciles Aeneas in Penrose.[12] His native background appears more substantially only as

>   this far-pitched, perilous, hostile place,
>   This solitary, hard-assaulted spot,
>   Fixed at the friendless, utter verge of space.[13]

But the note of hostility, it should be observed, does not extend to the inhabitants; the poem pleads for brotherhood among the beleaguered. At this stage Mason was morose but not misanthropic.

No New Thing (1934) marked the next and culminating phase of Mason's development. Though unnoticed at the time, it was also a landmark in the history of New Zealand verse. The technical proficiency of this collection, its scrupulous and consistent care for the poetic craft, set a standard which had never before—and has rarely since—been equalled. Formally the verse disclosed no startling innovations: as earlier, the sonnet and the quatrain occurred most frequently, an appearance of experimental novelty being due merely to typographical devices and the sparing use of both capitals and punctuation. These conventions may have been adopted in emulation of Latin poetry which in other ways has been a powerful influence on Mason's work, a constant source of imagery and reference. As disclosed in these poems, however, Mason's Rome is far removed from the Rome of Catullus and Horace; it is a city of 'rape and burn and pillage' —Rome of the primitive annalists or Christian martyrs.[14] On the first page of the collection, the poet himself dourly characterizes his 'bitter verses' as

> *sponges steeped in vinegar*
> *useless to the happy-eyed*
> *but handy for the crucified.*[15]

With a grim, self-probing, self-mortifying tenacity of purpose he proceeds to evoke a private hell of unfulfilled or rejected love, of strangulating parental affection, of dissolution, decay, and betrayal. Where a ray of light flickers through this gloomy abyss it comes from the gloating humour of 'Lugete Veneres' or the Christian charity of 'On the Swag'.

In the small quantity of verse he has published since 1934, Mason has occasionally voiced a desire to break out of the dark obsessional world of *No New Thing*. He writes in *End of Day* (1936),

> *I'll escape*
> *these charnel-clothes and I'll shape*
> *fresh selves under other skies. . . .*[16]

'Flow at Full Moon', included in *This Dark Will Lighten* (1941), does suggest some new and satisfying phase of experience, but it remains unique in Mason's work, a love poem expressing fulfilment and a deep sense of harmony with nature. Most of his later verse has been dedicated to the revolutionary cause which has proved no more amenable to him than to the majority of poets. *Squire Speaks* (1938) reads like a sketchy caricature of Auden and Isherwood, while the humane sentiments of *China* (1943) fail to compensate for the banality of its verse. Mason was the supreme poetic casualty in the political strife of the thirties.

For most of that troubled decade the loose alliance of the two Auckland poets was paralleled in Christchurch by a partnership between their younger contemporaries, Allen Curnow and Denis Glover. Curnow is that rarity among writers, a poet whom it is profitable to discuss in terms of influences—and one speaks the more certainly because he himself has been most generous in acknowledgment to persons and sources. A leading member of the *Phoenix* group, he seems to have served his poetic apprenticeship to Mason; certainly in formal respects his first collection, *Valley of Decision* (1933), owed something to the older poet, though the strained and turbid verses had none of Mason's directness and none of his intensity. More fruitful was the association with Glover, of which the first substantial outcome was *Enemies* (1937). Included in the book were two ambitious sequences and a group of satirical poems aimed at the scenes and denizens of urban New Zealand. The verse was carefully fashioned, intensely cerebral, rather tentative, as if the writer were feeling his way towards a personal manner and a congenial subject. In *Not in Narrow Seas* (1939), a poetic sequence with prose commentary, the subject and with it the fitting manner made their appearance. Possibly aided, as an epigraph suggests, by J. C. Beaglehole's *Short History* (1936), Curnow had found in the New Zealand past a theme worthy of his maturing talent. The approach was still satiric (or, more accurately, critical), but in place of the too-obvious targets of *Enemies*—mechanization, urban squalor, suburban banality—Curnow now wrote of a lost or mis-shapen destiny, of a petty race in sublime surroundings:

> *Two islands pointing from the Pole, upward*
> *From the Ross Sea and the tall havenless ice:*
> *Small trade and no triumph, men of strength*
> *Proved at football and in wars not their own.* . . .[17]

Having discovered his *métier* and finally discarded satire, Curnow proceeded to publish with a copiousness and a variety unequalled by any of his contemporaries. His meditations on the

New Zealand past (including the recent past) were next presented in *Island and Time* (1941), a loose poetic sequence of which the unifying element and presiding genius was 'Time':

> *I, more than your conscious carrier,*
>
> *Am island, am sea, am father, farm, and friend,*
> *Though I am here all things my coming attend;*
> *I am, you have heard it, the Beginning and the End.*[18]

That is straining the capacity of any secular abstraction, and the best parts of the sequence are those in which the devouring personification asserts its presence least insistently: the lyrics or the complex and moving 'Crash at Leithfield' or 'Country School'. The last, with its closely observed detail ('Scrub-worn floors and paint all peeled'), represents a kind of poem in which Curnow excels.[19] Some specific New Zealand feature or scene—a seascape, a building, a mountain landscape—becomes the vehicle for often intricate reflections on mutability and memory and human transience. A notable example of the *genre* is the title piece of *At Dead Low Water* (1949). With *The Axe*, published in the same year, Curnow extended his range into the field of drama. The tragedy is based on a recorded incident, the clash of two factions, Christian and pagan, in the island of Mangaia. Curnow is more concerned with the contemporary than with the historical aspects of this incident and, mainly through the agency of a chorus, he has attempted to convey its relevance to our time. The play suffers from the lack of established conventions in the poetic drama, but it is an original work, further witness to the writer's serious and tireless experimentalism.

The note of vaticination in *The Axe* finds no sympathetic echo in the work of Denis Glover. Throughout his career he has shunned anything savouring of the prophetic or the portentous. The youngest of the group, he was in the thirties the *enfant terrible* of New Zealand letters—a role for which he was qualified both by years and temperament, a role, moreover, which he has never brought himself wholly to relinquish. For more than twenty years a stream of good-humoured lampoons and well-turned epigrams has issued from his successive presses, enlivening and disinfecting the poetic scene. His youthful *Arraignment of Paris* (1937), aimed at a group of native poetesses and their impresario, remains the one piece of sustained literary satire produced in this country. He himself has never issued anything in the nature of a manifesto—such a proceeding would have been wholly out of character—but the early 'Home Thoughts' presents in concrete and succinct form a profession of poetic aims rather similar to Fairburn's:

> *I do not dream of Sussex downs*
> *Or quaint old England's quaint old towns:*
> *I think of what will yet be seen*
> *In Johnsonville and Geraldine.*[20]

For a brief interval the future of Johnsonville and Geraldine appeared to be bound up with that of a wider political territory roseate in hue: 'All of These' in its original version, for example, conjures up 'the new state', where lives will be ' "endless and singing joy" '.[21] Such a conception could not long survive the scrutiny of Glover's sceptical good sense; 'the new state' reappears in 'Lines on a Radical Meeting':

> *What think you, hungry-hearted ones, scrap-fed with words?*
> *Out of the tobacco smoke of the intellectuals*
> *The new state will rise?*[22]

What has survived from the thirties is Glover's sympathy with the great nameless majority once termed (but not by him) 'the toiling masses'. A craftsman himself, he has a special feeling for those who work with hands and brain—mechanics, engineers, artisans, pilots of sea and air—and it is noticeable that 'The Road Builders', a tribute to the 'unremembered legion' of New Zealand's navvies and engineers, opens his completest collection, *The Wind and the Sand* (1945). In this and a few related poems— ' "Scab-Loaded!" ', 'Root, and Crop, and Stone', 'Girls in a Factory'—he has given expression to the deepest and most enduring of democratic sentiments. His sympathy extends to the eccentrics and failures, to the bar-haunting veteran, the wandering shepherd, the naval deserter turned beach-comber. The fictitious mouthpiece of *Sings Harry* (1951), the dryly oracular bard with his old guitar, embodies many attributes of this class: he is reminiscent, gently cynical, mildly lecherous, turning finally not to his fellow-men but to nature. *Arawata Bill* (1952) elevates the solitary, nature-seeking eccentric to the status of folk-hero. Bill was an historical character, a gold-prospector who passed his life searching for the elusive lode. In a sequence of poems, stripped of superfluous verbiage, Glover presents his hero in characteristic scenes: Bill setting up camp or crossing a river; Bill with his pack-horse; Bill seen through the eyes of a barmaid; Bill at the end of his search:

> R.I.P. *where no gold lies*
> *But in your own questing soul*
> *Rich in faith and a wild surmise.*[23]

The work has an effect out of all proportion to its modest limits; the implications are those of epic.

Glover's best work has been done since 1940 (and here mention must be made of the small but impressive group of poems which came out of his war experience). Of Curnow it might also be said that the thirties were prentice years, while not until 1952 was Fairburn's poetic status fully revealed. Mason alone added little to his poetic achievement after 1940. These facts notwithstanding, the four poets had already made their presence felt by the middle thirties. Partly through their example, partly for other reasons in a complex situation, New Zealand's poetic climate had noticeably altered in the later years of the decade. The change was reflected even by mature writers of established reputation. Eileen Duggan, for instance, seems to have gained in her later work from the more rigorous conceptions of the poetic which penetrated her habitual seclusion. Striking also was the appearance in Alan Mulgan's *Aldebaran* (1937) of 'Success' which in mood and technique was fully in accord with the spirit of the times. With its slow, relentless rhythm and arid imagery, the poem (whose merit it took a poet, James K. Baxter, to recognize) is something more than an ironic elegy on one business magnate; it comments on a way of life and a society. In mordancy it surpasses J. C. Beaglehole's more explicit 'Meditation on Historic Change' (*Art in New Zealand*, September 1934), which in its opening sections expressed the sense of bankruptcy widely felt in the early thirties. The same writer's *Words for Music* (1938) is a more satisfactory work, giving some measure of the interests which have done so much, in so many ways, to enrich the life of contemporary New Zealand.

J. R. Hervey is a poet who, coming late to the literary arena, benefited from the innovations of his younger contemporaries—not exclusively or even mainly his New Zealand contemporaries; for he is somewhat detached from the local scene and appears to have escaped the contagion of nationalism. 'Salute to Youth' in *Selected Poems* (1940) was, in some sort, both acknowledgment of debt and pledge of allegiance. The middle-aged tyro emphatically turned from 'the old men', with their 'rich garrulity', to align himself with the young.[24] Despite this initial profession, Hervey's poetry is indeed a poetry of maturity and age—meditative in substance, quietist in mood, sometimes, yes, partaking of a 'rich garrulity'. It is in the main a poetry of the fireside and the study, prompted by legend or anecdote met with in discursive reading, by portentous happenings in the great world beyond, or —at its best—by events in a tranquil existence circumscribed by domesticity and devoted to good works. That such a life is not wanting in material for poems of modest scope and attainment is demonstrated throughout Hervey's three earliest collections; that it may also yield occasion for profounder poetry is attested by his latest, *She Was My Spring* (1954). In this volume, dedicated to his dead wife, Hervey has written a poetic sequence of rare distinction. The poems traverse the range of elegiac emotion and are grouped in series differing widely in mood and style: some resound in the grand hyperbolic seventeenth-century manner; others, more muted, flow in unrhymed verse; others again take form in a poignant lyricism. Poems loosely related to the central sequence are interspersed between each group. But always the poet returns to the theme of death:

> *This death in life, this empty calm,*
> *This riddle of your renouncing arm:*
> *This doom in depth love's counterpart....*[25]

It is as if he had traced the motions of grief as they ebb and flow in the living heart.

The setting of his native South Island rarely enters Hervey's poems and then only in rather vague terms, as if it lay somewhere towards the edge of his consciousness. In this respect, he stands in contrast to that other elegiac poet of Canterbury, Mary Ursula Bethell. Also a late-comer to literature, she published in 1929 *From a Garden in the Antipodes*, a collection which originated in verses sent to an English correspondent. Intimate, earthy, urbane, the poems celebrated the quiet round of horticultural enterprise and domestic incident in the writer's home on the Cashmere Hills, Christchurch. Some made their impact with the stylized precision of a Chinese ideograph, others achieved their effect of sophisticated humour by presenting a mundane subject in sonorous rhythms and elaborate phraseology. Recurring throughout the poems was a note of exile, heightened perhaps by the circumstances of their composition. And the poet's gaze sometimes wandered from the vegetable plot or the rose-bed to the distant mountains and she meditated on nature and time and the impermanence of our 'small fond human enclosures'.[26] Here Ursula Bethell introduced the themes of her later poetry; to quote from Helen M. Simpson's foreword to the *Collected Poems* (1950), hers was 'a continued attempt to express in living words the New Zealand, and especially the Canterbury, landscape, and what for the author lay at the heart of it, its implications in geological and temporal history, in time and in eternity'.[27] To the accomplishment of this immense task Ursula Bethell summoned all the formidable resources of her learning and vocabulary. Her approach to landscape was not by way of simple description or rhapsody, the method of previous New Zealand poets; she was not a 'word-painter'. It was as if she sought rhythmic and verbal equivalents for the particular scene before her, almost as if, like a sculptor, she were choosing her 'medium'.

Hence the endless variety and range of her metres, hence her employment of 'unpoetic' words when these best served her purpose. Her method was peculiarly well adapted to nature on the grand scale or in violent mood, as

> Bronze tussocked terraces before precipitous
> Great purple alps, loose glacier-shed
> Fierce-laughing streams in circuitous riverbed.[28]

or

> Yet still I hear the thunder of the waves' blind battering . . .
> I fear the hunger of the undertow, the sucked stones' hiss . . .[29]

At her weakest, it seemed that she had resolved to be a poet through sheer force of will and intellect, and her incantatory lines rolled on with an effect of intolerable monotony. In the elegiac mode she excelled not in commemorating the loss that lay nearest her heart but in the more generalized 'Long Harbour', a poem which alone would ensure remembrance for the name of Ursula Bethell.

Robin Hyde also holds a secure place in the poetic record, though the fact was not clearly apparent until the publication, more than a decade after her death, of *Houses by the Sea* (1952). Her earlier collections, of which *Persephone in Winter* (1937) was the fullest, expressed a genuine sensibility misdirected by habits she had acquired as a schoolgirl prodigy and later in the routine of popular journalism. Only towards the end of her life did she break through the shell of facile habit and romantic affectation to release a true poetic self. In a memoir prefixed to the posthumous volume, Gloria Rawlinson notes that late in 1936 Robin Hyde began to discard exotic themes and draw on New Zealand material. From this new phase came her finest work, 'Houses by the Sea.' The sequence, Miss Rawlinson explains, was begun in Auckland and completed overseas; like 'Journey from New Zealand', it may therefore owe some of its peculiar poignant intensity to the effects of absence. In conception it is a return to the past, a loving—but not sentimental—evocation of the writer's childhood in Wellington. The work opens appropriately with a group of poems, 'The Beaches,' set in the hot, endless summer of adult retrospection; thence it moves, in 'The Houses', to the more confined surroundings of suburbia, and passes to its conclusion in 'The People'. Skilfully combining narrative verse with lyric, thus effecting quick transitions in tempo and theme, the poet recreates the small complex world of her youth—the background of sea and hill and sky, the physical sensations, the emotional discoveries, the moments of terror and precocious intuition. One of her special achievements is in the sharply etched glimpses of the middle-class home:

> *Oven, gas-light and sink,*
> *The cracked plates getting hot,*
> *The tired man's tedious return*
> *To the house that honours him not.*[30]

Most notable of all is the portrait of the mother who appears briefly in the two previous sections and finally dominates 'The People':

> *one day*
> *Her eyes weren't tired, but weak; she still kept on*
> *A while yet, till our frocks were out of school:*
> *Poor old machine! I think it pricked a fool*
> *Heart-deep, a million times. . . .*[31]

In reading the sequence, one is constantly reminded of Katherine Mansfield's stories. It is not a matter of derivation but of a related approach by two writers to rather similar material, so that 'The Beaches' carries with it undertones of 'At the Bay', 'The Houses' subtle suggestions of *Prelude*, 'The People' faint echoes of 'New Dresses'. The effect is one of multiple associations, common enough in an older civilization, extremely rare in New Zealand; there is the sense of a literary tradition—only incipient, as yet limited and precarious, but still a tradition.

Walter D'Arcy Cresswell is a writer who stands apart from this or indeed any local tradition. 'Caught between an old order and a new anarchy,' wrote A. R. D. Fairburn, he retreated 'within the walls of a strongly fortified individualism'.[32] There he has remained, a figure of singular and heroic determination, who throughout a long career has neither hedged nor compromised in the propagation of opinions repugnant to most of his countrymen. For, as he chose the romantic writers of the nineteenth century to be his early mentors, so Cresswell embraced a romantic conception of the poet as bard, seer, legislator. His considered view, expressed in all his later work but most fully elaborated in *Eena Deena Dynamo* (1936), is that poets alone can save the modern world debauched since the time of Copernicus by science and reason. The messianic note has asserted itself gradually. It was scarcely heard in the early *Poems* (1928) or in its revised successor. Instead, amongst much that was too ambitious or weakly derivative, there was sometimes audible a voice of Blake-like simplicity and directness:

> *Plant thou in a poet's heart*
> *One dear word or look or deed,*
> *As the oak excels its seed*
> *So it will increase with Art.*
>
> *On that dark and holy ground*
> *Didst thou drop one silent tear,*
> *In the season of the year*
> *Something mighty will be found.*[33]

They are modest lines, their dress is unfashionable, and they falter; but they are genuine poetry, expressing—without preaching—a conception of the poetic office that is dignified and true. Here, moreover, as elsewhere both in verse and prose, the antique forms come to be accepted as essential elements in Cresswell's style, witnesses to a resolute habit of retrospection. The archaisms, then, cease to obstruct; not so, alas, the views they present with monotonous iteration. The views began to invade the verse in *Lyttelton Harbour* (1936) without, however, seriously marring that sequence which contains Cresswell's maturest and most accomplished poetry; they are responsible for the worst passages in *The Forest* (1952) (noble though that 'comedy' is in intention); and they have contributed to the tedious verbosity of *The Voyage* (1956). Similar views also appear in Cresswell's two exercises in autobiography, *The Poet's Progress* (1930) and *Present Without*

Leave (1939). But there they have a subordinate place and find their own correctives: for example, the views on women (carried to a grotesque extreme in *The Forest*) meet their fitting answer in the procession of patronesses, wise and disinterested, who pass through those two remarkable volumes; an even more eloquent reply is the sympathetic biography of Margaret McMillan (1948). These works, the autobiographies more especially, exhibit qualities obscured by the didacticism of Cresswell's later verse—his wit, his courage, his compassion, his marvellous candour.

Throughout the thirties Auckland was the centre of New Zealand prose-writing to an even greater extent than it was of poetry. An Aucklander by adoption, John A. Lee, first introduced to fiction an urban proletariat which had existed for most of New Zealand's history, though seldom recognized by its writers. On its publication in 1934, *Children of the Poor* enjoyed a *succès de scandale* which placed undue emphasis on questions of little relevance to criticism; whether it was a good novel or a bad novel by literary standards was the one question that, for the most part, remained unasked and unanswered. It is, in fact, a question not altogether easy to determine. *Children of the Poor* contained too much unassimilated descriptive matter and too many passages of undisguised propaganda for it to be classed in the first rank of fiction. In these respects it marked a decline and a return to the period before Jane Mander. Neither Dunedin nor New Zealand itself was taken for granted, but had to be explained, presumably for the convenience of readers overseas. A moral that was already obvious had to be underlined as Mrs. Grossmann at her most didactic might have underlined it. On the other hand, the novel explored tracts of New Zealand experience never before touched, and in the absence of any local precedent, technical faults were perhaps inevitable. And the deficiencies of style and construction only mar *Children of the Poor*; they do not outweigh its great merits. It is infinitely more than a social document; its best episodes—the Riversdale interlude and the account of Albany Porcello's successive apprenticeships, to mention only two—have an imaginative quality which makes it the more regrettable that elsewhere the

Upton Sinclair in John A. Lee gets the upper hand of the Mark Twain.

Lee has never again risen to the level of his first novel. The next two, *The Hunted* (1936) and *Civilian into Soldier* (1937), both contain excellent passages and have their special interest in continuing the chronicle begun in *Children of the Poor*. With less injustice, however, they might be classed as documents, personal as much as social; for the danger of drawing freely on autobiographic sources (a danger held in check in the initial book by its wider scope) becomes apparent in the sequels. The narrative of a sensitive and courageous youth's development when exposed to injustice and brutality is, up to a point, worth telling; beyond that point lies the marsh of self-dramatization and self-pity which the author does not always avoid. There followed a crude exercise in wartime sensationalism, then in 1944 *Shining with the Shiner*. Here, in the chronicles of an old-time 'swagger', Lee found a subject ideally suited to his predilection for the social rebel and the vagrant. His sketches have the colloquial raciness of an earlier phase of New Zealand writing, and they are sometimes very funny; but one comments (pointlessly it may be), if only he had been more of a Mark Twain, more of a Denis Glover!

Auckland was also the scene of Robin Hyde's superhuman labours during the late thirties. In her two 'Starkie' novels she continued the exploration of New Zealand's social depths begun by Lee's *Children of the Poor*. *Passport to Hell* (1936) and its sequel, *Nor the Years Condemn* (1938), are amazing *tours de force*, and wonder at the writer's temerity in tackling the subject competes with admiration at her success in reconstructing the life of Douglas Stark and through his life the shifting panorama of New Zealand in the early decades of this century—the New Zealand that exchanged the uncouth simplicity of pre-1914 years for Cairo and Flanders, that came back to the riotous interlude of 'boom and bust', that knew the years of depression, the excitement of the 1935 election, and the shadow of another war. The broad outlines of the picture are filled in with minutely detailed strokes, so that some curious scholar a century hence will be able to draw from the novels particulars of changes in fashion, the ritual of prisons and two-up schools, the language of desultory yarning in *estaminets* and bars. Robin Hyde's power to evoke scenes and incidents of which she could have had no direct experience was prodigious, but sometimes the self-imposed restrictions became irksome and she fell back on reporting or introduced some highly intelligent commentator of a poetic cast of mind, like Sister Collins who wanders improbably through *Nor the Years Condemn*. Had she written nothing more than these two novels, Robin Hyde would have done much to satisfy the aspiration quoted in *Phoenix*, '"We are hungry for the words that shall show us these islands and ourselves; that shall give us a home in thought." '[34]

Robin Hyde's imaginative colonization of her country was not confined to the 'Starkie' chronicle. With *Check to Your King* (1936) she entered the perilous field of historical fiction and brought off a brilliant success with her portrait of the Baron de Thierry, an eccentric figure after her own heart. *Wednesday's Children* (1937), a venture into the even greater hazards of whimsical romance, was a more qualified success—if success it may be termed. The work doubtless sprang from deep emotional sources, but it is largely populated by a set of stock characters, its satire is clumsy, and it is further weakened by the unrestrained exercise of personal fantasy. In her last novel, *The Godwits Fly* (1938), she finally explored the familiar territory of her own experience, the middle-class home of 'Houses by the Sea'. Within the broader limits of fiction, she succeeded not only in recalling the minutiae of that past life but also in suggesting the representative character of the family. The Hannays, with their experience of the 1914 war and its unsettling aftermath, typify a generation; the see-saw of their social aspirations went on in a multitude of suburban households; and there, too, was nourished that further aspiration suggested by the title. For the godwits symbolize the New Zealanders 'brought up on bluebells and primroses and daffodils and robins in the snow', who 'must make the long migration, under a compulsion they hardly understand; or else be dissatisfied all their lives long.'[35] The theme is not worked out to the point of resolution in this novel, but an article written in the course of Robin Hyde's own long migration makes it clear that she had reached a stage of equilibrium between paralysing subjection to the prestige of England and strident nationalism. 'Remember us for this, if for nothing else,' she wrote, 'in our generation, and of our own initiative, we loved England still, but we ceased to be "for ever England". We became, for as long as we have a country, New Zealand.'[36]

Whether this sense of harmony would have been expressed in the prose of Robin Hyde's maturity cannot now be known, for her last book was *Dragon Rampant* (1939), which dealt with a struggle remote from the mild agitations of New Zealand nationalism. The truth embodied in her rhetoric was, however, affirmed by one other writer who made the long migration ending in early death. In *Report on Experience* (1947) John Mulgan describes how the 'faery England' of his youthful fancy was replaced by a more complex, more accurate image and how he, in turn, found his way to the elemental fact that he was a New Zealander. 'If you try to . . . forget the country of your youth, as I did for a long time,' he confessed, 'you will lose the fight and wither internally of homesickness.' The New Zealand he recalls in his opening chapter is 'the most beautiful country in the world', often presented in the terms, even in the very phrases used by his poetic compatriots: an ancient land 'quite untouched by men'; its 'rocks and mountains . . . worn smooth by south Pacific winds'; its beaches 'of white, wind-driven sand, covered with driftwood from all the Pacific seas'. And there is more than a touch of proud poetic idealization in his picture of the New Zealanders encountered in the Egyptian desert, who 'marched into history'.[37] Only a small part of Mulgan's testament dwells on the issue of his native allegiance. He, too, was caught up in the larger conflicts of our time, and the final allegiance he implicitly affirmed extended beyond the confines of a single country; his sympathies and his faith seem, like Fairburn's, to have lodged ultimately with common humanity, irrespective of origin or creed.

Mulgan lived to assert his rediscovered loyalties in only one work of the imagination, the novel *Man Alone* (1939). Here there was no idealization and no poetry, unless the poetry of nature and that of ordinary lives. Departing from the normal path of the expatriate, he returned not to commemorate a familiar background but to confront the 'odd and ugly facts' which, as he relates in the *Report*, had come up to meet him in the depression.[38] He explored a world of the underdog and the fugitive—the world of Albany Porcello and Douglas Stark—but he did so with a restraint and a technical accomplishment unknown to his predecessors. In the colloquial American manner adapted from Hemingway, he created the figure of Johnson, decanted him from an immigrant ship in the nineteen-twenties, and set him on the course that was to carry him through a large area of the Auckland province and an important segment of local history (notably the depression and its riots). Johnson moves from job to job, drifts into loose friendship or easy love, murders without intent, takes refuge in the ranges. He is the 'man alone', the solitary, rootless nonconformist, who in a variety of forms crops up persistently in New Zealand writing—as the 'hatter' of mining yarns, as Philosopher Dick, as Arawata Bill, as the Shiner of Lee's sketches. In Mulgan's novel he also assumes a larger significance: he finally appears as a veteran of the Spanish Civil War, one of those men, a commentator remarks, that 'you can't kill'.[39] Johnson stands for the patient indestructible mass of humanity, borne along on the stream of history, perhaps in the end determining its direction.

Just as *Report on Experience* supplements Mulgan's novel, so Roderick Finlayson's *Our Life in this Land* (1940) provides an illuminating gloss on his successive works of fiction. In that essay, he proclaimed himself one of Cresswell's disciples, an opponent of modern scientific civilization. Looking back on the course of New Zealand history, he saw it not as a record of progress but as one of decline from the state of comparative harmony achieved by the pioneers. Such views lie behind most of Finlayson's fiction, influencing—though never rigidly determining—his choice of themes and characters. Already in 1938 he had published *Brown Man's Burden*, a collection of stories and sketches of contemporary Maoris. Here the thesis was forcefully illustrated: the Maoris were shown as despoiled and degraded by European influence while they still retained certain of their primitive, 'poetic' virtues.[40] The contrast was often presented through two sets of characters—on one hand the uncorrupted elders, on the other a younger generation led astray by emulation of the *pakeha*. In 'The Totara Tree', where Maoris were directly opposed to Europeans, the conflict was centred on two objects, the sacred birth tree and the electric power pole, which took on symbolic significance. No other story could compare with that small masterpiece, but the whole collection was notable for an approach to Maori life which combined sympathetic insight with realism; and, theory notwithstanding, the final impression was less of corruption than of abounding vitality. The odour of corruption was more marked in the Maori sketches of *Sweet Beulah Land* (1942), especially those set in the squalor of Auckland's slums and Chinese market gardens, though even there Finlayson detected acrid humour and twisted affection. As a whole, this collection was less of a piece than its predecessor, satire mingling with humour, rural sketches with somewhat contrived demonstrations of the thesis.

The thesis has a prominent part in *Tidal Creek* (1948), a loosely connected series of sketches of a rural settlement in the Auckland province. Tidal Creek is isolated, backward, largely self-sufficient, a stronghold of the pioneer virtues which are expounded to the hero Jake by his eccentric Uncle Ted. The book contains an abundance of bucolic humour, some shrewd rustic wisdom, and an excessive number of picturesque characters and often pointless incidents. A more serious and unified work is *The Schooner Came to Atia* (1952). In accordance with the mood of the times—or perhaps simply through a change of scene— Finlayson has here relegated his former interests to a minor place. Though the shortcomings of western civilization are mentioned in conversation, they have no essential part in the drama of Europeans and natives on a small Pacific island. That drama is largely a personal one, its reverberations moral and psychological rather than social. The three main characters are given verisimilitude as creatures of time and place; but more fundamentally they are frail human beings, caught up in an immemorial situation which the author presents with impartiality and compassion.

Finlayson's work is often so good, occasionally so profound that one is puzzled by its failure to amount, in the total, to something more impressive. A tangible answer to a complex question lies in the writer's indifference to the refinements of his chosen form. His fiction reveals small interest in technique and of external influence scarcely a trace. Thus in presenting Maori speech he usually adopts a convention current in journalism for half a century, the staccato English sentence, sprinkled with 'Ehoas!' and 'Py korrys!' Though the convention works, it imperfectly represents the original, and at times it betrays the author into a condescending attitude that is far removed from his intentions. This acceptance of the ready-made, together with other features of Finlayson's writing—the loose ends, the solecisms, the homespun philosophy—blunt the force of his fiction and weaken the impact of his massive integrity. Artlessness has its own virtues and its own peculiar strength; but in the long run it is no substitute for art.

If one speaks of art in reference to contemporary New Zealand fiction, that is largely due to the achievement of Frank Sargeson. More than two decades have now passed since there appeared in *Tomorrow* a series of sketches later collected in *Conversation with my Uncle* (1936). The contents of that small pamphlet bore the clear imprint of their time and first place of publication: superficially they were 'radical' in their purport, attacking or questioning the assumptions of bourgeois society. But where *Tomorrow's* contributors usually made a frontal assault on war or capitalist economics or middle-class morality, Sargeson approached them by a method of indirection. An issue was reduced to the simplest terms and set forth in a kind of dramatic monologue; in the title sketch, for instance, monopoly capitalism was presented through the homely image of bananas at a picnic. Besides the moral and political fables, there were two sketches more closely resembling normal 'stories', 'Sketch from Life' (later retitled 'A Good Boy') and 'I've Lost my Pal'. The first introduced one of Sargeson's recurring characters, the 'good', well brought up boy who breaks away from his respectable parents; the second entered the society of rural workers and shearers, the 'proletariat', here bearing little resemblance to the noble abstraction of intellectual debate. It is plainer now than it was in the thirties that New Zealand literature had acquired not a conforming 'leftist' but that less docile radical, an artist. Sargeson's artistry was again less obvious at the outset, though to discerning eyes it was already apparent. As a medium for his deceptively naïve approach, he used a simple, colloquial English based on New Zealand speech and adapted in each sketch to the character of the monologist. He was not the first writer to employ the local idiom, but none of his predecessors had shown so sensitive an ear for the rhythms and vocabulary of everyday speech, and none had learned so much from the American masters.

The sketches and stories collected in *A Man and his Wife* (1940) disclosed a notable advance in technique. The colloquial monologue, still the predominant form, had now been shaped into a far more flexible medium, working at its best with the allusive economy of poetry. This subtle art had been developed not, of course, as an end in itself but as a means for expressing a wider and profounder view of life. The new collection included sensitive studies of childhood and in 'Three Women' of young womanhood; the settings ranged from small town to rural slum, while on one notable occasion the scene was European; the characters numbered factory-workers, struggling farmers, minor public servants, racecourse hands. Sargeson's world at this period was largely that of the social underling, his chief preoccupations the lusts and fancies and strange affections that lie hidden in obscure recesses of the human heart. This phase of his work, finely expressed in such stories as 'The Making of a New Zealander' and 'An Affair of the Heart', culminated in *That Summer* (1946), a collection which drew its title from a *nouvelle*. 'That Summer' remains Sargeson's most satisfying story, beautifully proportioned and nearly always convincing: the down-at-heel urban *milieu* is superbly evoked, and through the eyes of the hero-narrator the characters take shape with a Defoe-like actuality. Occasionally the prose is opaque with esoteric slang, and the homosexual sub-plot is clumsily devised; but these flaws apart, skill is here triumphantly united with understanding.

I Saw in my Dream (1949) elaborated to novel length the subject of an early sketch: Sargeson took the son of middle-class, church-going parents and traced his moral pilgrimage through childhood and youth to the point of emancipation. The work is rich in incidentals. A whole era of history passes before the reader's eyes, the minutiae of life in New Zealand town and country during the early decades of this century. Alas, the strength of a novel does not lie in its incidentals, nor in its contribution to social history. *I Saw in my Dream* lacks any unifying theme except the groping struggle of the hero, Henry-Dave, who is too negative a figure to excite interest, much less compassion. Periodic failure—and the failure of this novel is qualified and only relative—is one of the hazards that beset a writer who works without the support of tradition, who is indeed the forger of tradition. Sargeson has since returned to the *nouvelle* form and opened up new territory with *I for One* (1954). This comic and corrosive study of the realities lying behind the suburban façade does not differ greatly in intention from the sketches which, almost a generation ago, enlivened the pages of *Tomorrow*. But to compare the qualities of those stiff little fables with the multiple complexities and subtle ironies of the later work is to measure the extent of Sargeson's artistic growth in the intervening years. It is to recognize, moreover, that he has been consistently true to his personal vision and has cultivated to the full his native talent. Of no writer can more be expected.

Like all the significant novelists who emerged in the thirties, Sargeson is closely identified with Auckland. Throughout those fertile years, indeed, there came from the southern provinces only one writer of imaginative prose, and he made his appearance at the end of the decade, its critic, moralist, and commentator. M. H. Holcroft was also, it happened, a novelist, but a novelist *manqué*. In the course of the traditional grand tour of enterprising New Zealand youth, he had published two novels, and for a time after returning to Canterbury he continued the writing of fiction. His interests, however, gradually shifted to criticism, and soon after entering daily journalism he began work on a long essay of a kind unique in this country, though it has some parallels in the literature of New England. The new enterprise, Holcroft has explained, was prompted by a desire for self-expression that leader-writing could not satisfy and arose from his personal experiences and wide reading in the previous years. Withdrawn to the seclusion of New Zealand's southernmost centre, he devoted his leisure to the essay which was published in 1940 and became the first part of a trilogy finally collected under the title of *Discovered Isles* (1950).

The purpose of *Discovered Isles*, as the author himself has formulated it, was to examine 'the nature of creative problems in New Zealand'.[41] The subject of literature lies at the heart of the book, animating the separate essays and unifying the trilogy. Nevertheless, at numerous points it extends far beyond literary confines. With the growth of the work, its scope seems to have widened insensibly until it became, in effect, a study of New Zealand civilization. In so large an inquiry, touching so many fields, a uniform level of achievement could scarcely have been expected. Besides its insights and revelations, the work inevitably yields both lapses and *longueurs*. The least satisfactory sections occur when the writer assumes the two contrasting roles in his repertoire: when he indulges in the topicality of the leader-writer, or again when, as speculative essayist, he expounds some nebulous intuition. On the other hand, where his intuitive method is applied in elucidating the work of a poet, Holcroft is superlatively good. His studies of individual writers, especially those of Ursula Bethell and D'Arcy Cresswell, are milestones in our literature, the first criticism worthy of the name to appear in New Zealand. In the years since they were published, these critical interpretations have been immensely fruitful; nor is their seminal power yet at an end. The whole trilogy has, in fact, proved itself one of the most potent works of recent times, an influence—either as inspiration or irritant—on numerous minds. *Discovered Isles* stands alone not merely in New Zealand letters but in Holcroft's own writings: none of his other works before or since can compare with the three essays. Not for the first time, a peak in the personal development of a writer coincided with a culminating point in his country's history.

VIII

The Middle Decades

FROM the flat sceptical calm of the succeeding decade, one looks back with a certain feeling of nostalgia to the early nineteen-forties. They were years of war and war's disturbing sequel, but they were also years of assurance combined with expectation. A consciousness of achievement, fostered by the Centennial, had been strengthened by the exalted feats of New Zealand arms; at that time it seemed not vainglorious to believe that the nation had attained to some measure of maturity. The war, furthermore, had brought to this country, in common with others, not only a heightened sense of living but a heightened sense of the arts. Creative ambitions were pondered or discussed wherever New Zealanders were dispersed by the chance of war. In literature, the impulse of authorship, often stimulated by the writing of letters and the keeping of diaries, found expression in service newspapers and ephemeral war-time publications. These products of exotic presses and erratic leisure occasionally inspired a hope that the nascent tradition of the thirties would be continued and enriched by a new generation of writers, nurtured in depression, toughened by war. The unromantic verse, the sardonic sketches, the unvarnished tales of escape and privation gave promise, at their best, of a small realistic renascence in New Zealand writing.

With the end of war, the signs were even more propitious. A notable event in the opening year of peace was the appearance of Allen Curnow's *Book of New Zealand Verse 1923–45.* The anthology presented the results of a search through many fugitive publications, so that for the first time it was possible to appreciate the range and quality of the poetry written in the previous twenty years. To this critical service Curnow added still further by supplying an introduction where he surveyed the whole field of

New Zealand verse and extended the work of thematic interpretation begun by Holcroft. Here, defined and illustrated, was a poetic heritage which the post-war writers might, as talent and disposition determined, either accept or discard. At the end of the same year, 1945, the public-spirited Harry H. Tombs issued the first *Arts Year Book*, successor to *Art in New Zealand* and for its seven numbers a medium of publication for poets and essayists. Following Australian precedent, the State then made its own substantial contribution. A government, whose solicitude for the arts had been liberally displayed during the Centennial, set up in 1947 a literary fund to assist New Zealand writers. Thence has flowed a beneficent stream of grants, bringing in their train few, if any, of the evils commonly ascribed to official patronage of letters. Thus equipped with a small battery of special presses (soon to be supplemented by the Pegasus Press of Christchurch), an apparatus of criticism, and a source of patronage, New Zealand letters now acquired that essential desideratum, a periodical. Since its inception in 1939, the *New Zealand Listener* had reviewed local books and published the work of imaginative writers; but its principal concern was broadcasting, and the space it could use for literature necessarily limited. *New Zealand New Writing*, though it filled a war-time gap, had expired before passing beyond the phase of imitation; while *Arena*, that brave little venture founded in 1943, had small influence outside its narrow circle of intimates. The need was for a periodical of national scope, for 'the type of journal,' as Holcroft expressed it, 'which every serious writer dreams of . . . a journal devoted entirely to the arts.'[1] The dream was realized in March 1947 with the first issue of *Landfall*.

The longest lived and best produced literary periodical in New Zealand history was founded by its editor, Charles Brasch. So closely is he identified with *Landfall*, so strongly has he influenced its character and policy, that the periodical is best approached through a consideration of the editor. Chronologically, Brasch is a writer of the thirties. Though living abroad for many years, he seems to have been reluctant to lose touch with his native land and contributed to both *Phoenix* and *Tomorrow*. His literary career has throughout been closely bound up with New Zealand and, except for one work, all his publications bear a local imprint. The exception is *The Quest* (1946), words for a mime play. This experiment in poetic allegory presents through the figure of The Shepherd the search for a life that will reconcile 'The root of nature and the flower of man'. Here Brasch defines in generalized terms the quest for harmony that governs his own life, and he brings the play to a climax where the personal reference becomes obvious. After chastening experiences of the world, The Shepherd announces,

> *I have described a circle round the earth*
> *And reached my starting place,*
> *And I am ready for that which awaits me there.*[2]

The play, which was published on the eve of Brasch's return to New Zealand, had been preceded by *The Land and the People* (1939) and was followed by *Disputed Ground* (1948). In both collections a diffident, sensitive, painstaking talent is revealed, and at the core of each is a group of New Zealand poems, the outcome of two visits made during the thirties. The majority of these are nature poems, either evocations of specific scenes or more abstract meditations on landscape. Clearly Brasch was both attracted and repelled by the New Zealand environment: attracted by its naked grandeur (or in *Disputed Ground* by the aura of its Polynesian past), repelled by its untamed, alien character and the absence of historical and human associations. 'There are no dead in this land,' he reflects, 'No personal sweetness in its earth. . . .'[3] As he returned to his own 'starting place', his mood, like The Shepherd's, may well have been one of stoical submission to an uncertain future.

The next phase of the quest is a part of literary history, recorded both in the volumes of *Landfall* and in Brasch's latest work, *The Estate* (1957). Recurring throughout that collection is a note of harmony, a sense of reconciliation, suggesting that the poet has travelled far towards the end defined in his allegory. Even in the title sequence, where he returns again and again to confront the fact of individual separateness, the impression finally given is of a life rich in friendship and aesthetic satisfactions. Untamed nature, violence, human folly—they are there, but at the edge of the picture, seen from the ancestral groves of Thurlby Domain or from the refuge of Willi Fels's garden,

> *Where climates, continents, civilizations mingled*
> *And for a leaf-framed listening Apollo*
> *The bellbird lingered over its flawless phrases....*[4]

Only once does the alien element—not now in nature's guise—break through with all its intractable strength. Brasch takes sensual, sinning, shiftless man (Glover's or Sargeson's), characterizes him in metallic language, places him in history, and rejects him. 'Duri Miles Ulixi' is a powerful poetic statement, but through limited comprehension it falls short of the highest. *The Estate* is a superbly accomplished collection, product of a rare maturity. It fails, however, to reach the level of Fairburn, say, at his best; it excludes too much, its range of experience and sympathies is too narrow. *Landfall* is a magnificent achievement, every number testifying to the editor's impartiality, his skill, his standards of taste and judgment. The beautifully printed, scrupulously edited volumes, illustrated and analysed and indexed, merit nothing but gratitude and respect. Again, nevertheless, the carping, qualifying voice is raised: Need they have been so carefully pruned and cultivated? Could they not have found more space for the rank growth of experiment or the frail saplings of youthful self-expression? The answers must be in the negative. *Landfall* could have been different only by sacrificing its main source of strength, the principles of its editor. The response to its necessary limitations should have been other journals, different in scope and intention.

Recent years have, in fact, been relatively prolific in periodicals set up to supplement or emulate *Landfall* or, alternatively, as centres of mild disaffection. There were the shortlived *Hilltop* and *Arachne*; there is, latest incarnation of the radical *Phoenix*, *Here and Now*; there is the literary quarterly, *Numbers*; more substantially in a specialized field there is the *New Zealand Poetry Yearbook*, founded and edited by Louis Johnson. On its inception in 1951, the *Yearbook* promised—or threatened—to become a medium for younger poets writing in opposition to their elders: a spokesman, Erik Schwimmer, announced in the first number the rejection of 'the Curnow-Holcroft myth' of a 'lonely island-desert, discovered by navigators and developed by baffled explorers'; the new poetic generation, he implied, was turning away from 'the peculiarly New Zealand experience' to write a more abstract poetry reflecting 'the internationalization of culture'. The following year, the editor himself, with greater tact and clarity, put forward a similar case, but at the same time admitted there were no 'groups' and no 'specific tendencies' in New Zealand poetry, only 'men alone', 'poetic Crusoes'—a conclusion borne out by his varied and catholic choice. For in practice Johnson has ranged widely for his annual selection: he has included writers regardless of age or affiliation, and, from deliberate policy, has not insisted on a high level of accomplishment. 'It is both the strength and weakness of *Poetry Yearbook*,' he writes with candour, 'that its purpose is revelatory rather than definitive—to show, year by year, that which is growing rather than that which is fully-formed.'[5]

Johnson's editorial principles have apparently been applied in the publication of his own work. His aim, it would seem, has not been to exhibit the few carefully finished products of a poetic development but to present the process itself in all its abundance of preliminary drafts and constant experimentation. The result, as seen in three major collections and a number of lesser works, is, in its own manner, impressive. In spite of—or because of—the rough edges of technique and expression, the verse makes its impact with an urgent and arresting force. Johnson has followed the advice he gives to a nameless poet:

> *Let him be wild and irritate his skin*
> *With the disease of living—leaving his age*
> *Wailing its weals.* . . .[6]

Words in his hands become scourges both of analysis and communication. He is almost wholly a poet of the city and, to a less exclusive extent, a poet of personal relations. The two collections published in 1951, *The Sun among the Ruins* and *Roughshod among the Lilies*, are pervaded by a powerful sexuality, more often culminating in the self-tortured disillusion of Mason (a writer with whom Johnson has some temperamental affinity) than in the fulfilment of Fairburn's love poetry. In *New Worlds for Old* (1957) the sexual theme invades the traditional Eden of childhood remembrance and, in an expression of the poet's talent for grotesque humour, it penetrates to the vegetable garden. Johnson's latest work is most notable, however, for his emergence as a social critic and satirist, seen at his most effective in the grim quartette of 'Poems for the Strontium Age' with which the collection ends. There Johnson gives plausible shape to the cataclysm haunting his imagination in earlier poems, and there, with the irony of the times, the urban poet celebrates nature's healing power.

If Brasch and Johnson represent two extremes of editorial and poetic practice, the intermediate position is held by James K. Baxter. He is, indeed, the central figure in the contemporary scene, mediator among writers of different ages and outlooks, focus of highest hopes for the future. Not that he belongs in the category of the 'promising'; while still in his early thirties, his past as poet and critic is already substantial. In 1944 he published *Beyond the Palisade*, a collection which rightly won him a place in Curnow's anthology. The youthful poet appeared with ease in the company of his elders, and, on the evidence of such poems as 'Prelude N.Z.', could be counted their first brilliant disciple. Familiar themes—nature's menace, the spiritual strength of the Polynesians, the precariousness of European occupation—reappeared, acquiring fresh force through Baxter's matchless gift of phrase and lyric. This indigenous vein, with others exposed by the youthful virtuoso, might have occupied a lesser poet for the rest of his career. But Baxter has repeatedly been compelled to disappoint expectations, to follow not the predictable and approved course but the stonier path dictated by his own *daimon*. His next work, *Blow, Wind of Fruitfulness* (1948), was superficially less attractive than its predecessor, though it contained profounder poetry. It seemed to proceed from a state of spiritual depression, reflected in the images of winter pervading the collection and in the studied avoidance of rhetoric. In the interval between this and his next work, he made his appearance as a critic. *Recent Trends in New Zealand Poetry* (1951) was remarkable not merely for the maturity of its judgments but for its strong ethical bias. Poetry, Baxter affirmed, 'should contain moral truth,' every poet 'should be a prophet according to his lights', and should, further, be 'a cell of good living in a corrupt society'.[7] The garments of teacher and exemplar are not easily assumed in our times; and in his next collection, *The Fallen House* (1953), Baxter himself could supply no simple message to a distracted world. Instead, like Hart Crane, he mined 'the black gold / Of prophecy' from an experience that was often bitter and sometimes sordid; he praised and in his own person illustrated a 'passionate integrity'; and in one passage he proclaimed a noble aspiration:

> *We have one aim: to set men free*
> *From fear and custom and the incessant war*
> *Of self with self and city against city.* . . .[8]

Baxter's serious poetry has provided only one outlet for his copious energies. A critical study, *The Fire and the Anvil* (1955), and the parodies of *The Iron Breadboard* (1957) may be cited as further expressions of an intelligence which has flowed, with vitalizing results, into almost every branch of contemporary letters. Baxter's presence, in fact, goes far to explain why in recent years Wellington has become the most vigorous centre of New Zealand verse. An example of its lively iconoclasm is seen in *Poems Unpleasant* (1952) where, in the company of Baxter and Johnson, an older writer, Anton Vogt, has risen to a level of achievement far above that of his earlier publications. Neither in this collection, however, nor in his *Love Poems* (1952) does Vogt approach within measurable distance of his colleagues: agility in rhyming, superabundant gusto, and command of a large range of literary gestures cannot replace essential poetic attributes. Nor does it seem that Ruth Gilbert in *Lazarus* (1949) and *The Sunlit Hour* (1955) has yet achieved anything more profound than the poetry of good intentions. The buoyant fluency of her poems together with their profusion of ideas (dramatic, devotional, intimate, whimsical) make them faintly reminiscent of the early Robin Hyde; the future will show whether the author shares with her predecessor a mature capacity to confront experience without exploiting it for dubious literary ends.

Among writers who have responded with greater restraint to the poetic stimulus of the capital are Alistair Campbell and Pat Wilson. Campbell's *Mine Eyes Dazzle* (1950) and Wilson's *The Bright Sea* (1951) are the poetry of youth, but the phrase does not carry the connotations it might have done thirty years ago: there are no extravagant attitudes, no large, lax generalizations. Each poet has kept strictly within the confines of a limited talent, aiming at precision in communicating a narrow range of experience. Campbell is seen at his best in an elegiac sequence where a lithe grace of style enables him to encompass with ease a variety of modes, even the animistic hyperbole:

> *The shattered cliff's sheer*
> *Face spurts myriads*
> *Of waterfalls, like tears*
> *From some deep-bowed head....*[9]

Wilson's approach is more tentative and subdued; his quiet rhythms and limpid phrases aspire towards a form of symbolic utterance or, with greater success, present the outlines of a remembered sea-scape:

> *Evening, a lemon-yellow sunset*
> *And all the winds idle,*
> *That night, flat calms all down the coast*
> *And only the tides running....*[10]

Pupils of an exacting school, these writers have published sparingly since the appearance of their first collections; on present indications, the humorous self-knowledge, the warm humanity, and the superb virtuosity of Wilson's 'Staying at Ballisodare' (*Landfall*, December 1954) hold out greater promise of completely mature and perhaps profound achievement than Campbell's seasonal recensions and rearrangements of *Mine Eyes Dazzle*.

The two remaining members of the 'Wellington group' (to

adopt Baxter's tentative classification) profess an even more rigorous, indeed agonizing, conception of the poetic office.[11] In *Fire without Phoenix* (1957), W. H. Oliver opens a poem entitled 'Ceremony of Pain' with the invocation, 'Come with sufficient reverence to write; / The act's a sacrament.'[12] And the witty conceit that ends the collection identifies the poems with the few surviving escapees from a concentration camp. Similarly (but without wit) Hubert Witheford in *The Falcon Mask* (1951) depicts the poet 'Hounded towards the ritual he shuns', while elsewhere in the same work poetic utterances are termed 'sweaty strivings of the heart'.[13] The literary subject-matter, the air of tortured cerebration, the ritualistic imagery, with its anthropological reference, are all characteristic of the bookish and esoteric tendencies of much recent verse. In reading Witheford more especially, it is as if one were invited—or ceremonially challenged—to participate in painful but obscure mysteries whose inner purport is known only to the poet-priest himself. He has travelled far from the passionate lucidity of 'Elegy in the Orongorongo Valley' which graced *Shadow of the Flame* (1950):

> *Did death's lightning show him this shadowed valley*
> *Burning through oceans, green beyond time?*
> *Was this the river he felt closing over*
> *Islands of pain and over his life?*[14]

That early poem does, nevertheless, point forward to Witheford's later style, with its extreme contrasts and violent metaphors: there he conjures up a landscape of 'glowing ice' and 'burning tombs', of 'blackened cities' and 'congealed sea'; sleep is a 'mad terrain', a 'scalding river', love a 'funeral pyre' or, in milder terms, the 'unappeasable contest'.[15] Such linguistic excess, emphasized by the formal accomplishment of Witheford's verse, often mars the effect of serious poetry and, when indulged in throughout the greater part of a collection, is evocative not of primitive ritual but of modern melodrama. Oliver, too, deploys the familiar symbols of a bleak age—the 'self-inflicted wounds', the 'waste shore', the 'dry bones'—but he does so with discretion in a group of poems varied both in tone and content.[16] There are the occasional verses of the cultivated writer, his meditations on music, drama, history; there are literary fancies and exercises; there are trophies of the sensitive traveller; and, pre-eminently, there is 'In the Fields of my Father's Youth', a refined contribution to the long debate on colonial loyalties. As he reflects on his dual inheritance, Oliver makes no final commitment, but he does foresee the 'breaking point'

> *where loyalties depart and go their ways*
> *separate, hostile, taking up their arms*
> *to meet in battle on the disputed field*
> *of England's and our own heart's heritage.*[17]

The long debate, it may be added, has entered still another phase with *A Splinter of Glass* (1956) by Charles Doyle, a post-war migrant who traces in the title sequence his experience of social and spiritual adaptation. Clothing his theme in the allusive, recondite, 'international' garb, the writer has produced an interesting work; had he chosen to write as directly as elsewhere in the collection, his poem might have been comparable with Oliver's.

The 'Auckland group' is a term which, if not authorized by Baxter, finds some justification in facts. Mary Stanley, M. K. Joseph, Kendrick Smithyman, and Keith Sinclair comprise a loosely knit association of writers, while at a distance Gloria Rawlinson divests herself of habits and reputation acquired in childhood. The members of the central group, though differing in poetic aims and practice, are linked by interests which, in a union somewhat rare in New Zealand, combine the domestic with the academic. A favourite theme of Auckland verse is the metaphysics of the married state, common forms of poetic utterance are the connubial compliment and the filial invocation. More reticent than his younger associates (schooled, moreover, in another discipline of self-revelation), Joseph is sparing of poetic intimacies. Much of the work collected in *Imaginary Islands* (1950) is the by-product of a scholar's reading and reflection—the epigram, the parody, the erudite pastiche, the nonsense rhyme. To this almost virgin province of local letters, as to his satirical and occasional pieces, Joseph has brought the resources of a witty, cultivated mind. Even his more personal poetry often has its origin in literary preoccupations or is coloured by them: 'The Lovers and the City' (*Landfall*, September 1953) is not merely a highly accomplished poem but also a work of scholarship; and a literary allusion is introduced with telling effect into the ironic 'Victory March':

> *I shall see children playing in the rubble of a street*
> *And a girl who turned to folly for a tin of meat*
> *I shall hear an old man weeping by a broken door*
> *And I shan't sleep so easy as the lads who march no more.*[18]

Sinclair is another versatile scholar-poet who not infrequently assumes the part of *pasticheur* and also turns from more arduous labours to the composition of nonsense verse. Rarely, however, is he a practitioner of the latter *genre* in its purest form; at the core of his inconsequential jingles may usually be discovered some fragment of personal sentiment or natural observation. The best of *Songs for a Summer* (1952), for example, conjure up with an immediacy hardly possible in more lucid verse the languorous, anarchic atmosphere of the sub-tropical north at certain seasons. Among Auckland poets he is most responsive to landscape and the subtle inward essence of place. 'Ihumatao' with similar poems in *Strangers or Beasts* (1954) render for perhaps the first time in New Zealand verse the peculiar mingling of lush farmland and tidal wilderness that characterizes the Auckland peninsula:

> *Here the long waves of grass break,*
> *Checked by the mud's acres, where strange*
> *Cows pasture in the sea-grass,*
> *Chewing their salt cud on the meadows*
> *Of mud. . . .*[19]

In his imaginative exploration of the past, Sinclair's outstanding work is 'Memorial to a Missionary', harmonious outcome of partnership between historian and poet, anthropologist and artist. There, too, his feet stand firmly on native ground.

Smithyman, by contrast, is the least local of writers. The

setting of his poetry, more often than not, is the austere landscape of contemporary myth; the fauna that throng his sad fables are creatures of symbolic substance; the themes of his verse, unless they are personal, are usually drawn from the art and literature of Europe. He is, in short, an exponent of that poetic Esperanto known as the international style; and it is a misfortune for his reputation that in *The Blind Mountain* (1950), the one major collection he has thus far published, the style should so consistently appear at its most impenetrable. Not that Smithyman's is intentionally 'private' poetry. In the beautiful but obscure poem that opens the book, he expresses 'the green trembling wish to speak across our age'.[20] That aim (with its characteristic tinge of ambiguity) comes closer to realization in the work that has appeared since 1950; but, whether in this age or the next, the audience reached by his elliptical, highly finished verse is likely to be confined to connoisseurs of the devious and the erudite. In less accomplished minds, the appeal, 'put down Spinoza, Pericles / the seventeenth century', stirs a sympathetic response.[21] The affectionately satiric plea comes from *Starveling Year* (1952) by Mary Stanley whose poetry on occasion yields its own complexities. These, however, do not arise from calculated density of style or excess of learning but rather from the attempt to convey a view of things that is at once complex and profound. It is a view that comprehends the ecstasy of love and the pain, that sees both the innocence of childhood and its darker potentialities, that embraces the Ariel in human nature together with the Caliban. Basically it is a Christian conception of life, and, as presented by Mary Stanley, its terms are always feminine. With an emotional maturity exceedingly rare in our literature, she speaks as wife, mother, daughter, proclaiming but never exploiting the qualities of her sex:

> *Being a woman, I am*
> *not more than man nor less*
> *but answer imperatives*
> *of shape and growth.*[22]

The words might be pondered by Gloria Rawlinson who, in her

brave efforts to reshape an earlier over-feminine style, tends (on the evidence of scattered pieces) to suppress the deeper imperatives.

Turning from the North Island, one first encounters the city of Christchurch which publishes poetry in abundance but now, it would seem, rarely nurtures poets. For in the years since 1940 the main southern centre has produced few writers of talent; and the most substantial of these, Basil Dowling, belongs to the generation of the thirties rather than to their successors. His first book of poems, *A Day's Journey* (1941), recorded in enduring terms sentiments that were familiar to a majority of his thoughtful contemporaries and led courageous spirits to prisons and detention camps. Intense convictions and the circumstances of the time thus compelled him for a brief period to adopt the role of social critic. Born into a happier age, he would not have been deflected from the part for which talent and temperament have fitted him—that of nature and devotional poet in the purest English tradition. Though not ignored in *Signs and Wonders* (1944) and *Canterbury* (1949), injustice, strife, the mysteries of pain and evil have a subordinate place. In those later collections, Dowling most often writes of nature, for preference nature in its gentler aspects; or he turns to childhood, finding there a lost 'Elysium of innocence'; or he attests his uncomplicated faith:

> *What says the soul of Death*
> *And his huge crime?*
> *Soul says, I save my breath*
> *And bide my time.*[23]

Neat craftsmanship and distinction of phrasing give freshness to his handling of familiar themes; and, in general, he avoids Georgian triviality because his simplicity is natural, not assumed.

Diverse styles are nowhere more clearly illustrated than in the three writers who share with Dowling the poetic terrain of Canterbury. Paul Henderson, Charles Spear, and W. Hart-Smith are alike solely in their use of metrical language as a medium for intermittent self-expression. The publication of Paul Henderson's *Unwilling Pilgrim* in 1955 marked the advent of an exceptionally gifted recruit to the ranks of the South Island metaphysicals. The writer (who first published under the name of Ruth France) might be broadly termed a nature poet; but to an even smaller extent than Ursula Bethell, her spiritual forbear and occasional preceptress, does she concern herself with nature to the exclusion of man. She draws from her rock garden the text for a moral fable; her finely observed landscapes lead her on to subtle self-communings or to reflections on the issues of life and conduct; she evokes a magnificent sea-scape which she peoples with the ghostly presences of her forerunners. She is humanist before she is nature-lover; her themes are the eternal ones firmly based on the particular and the local. Spear, by contrast, is tenuously linked with the Canterbury scene. His exotic eclecticism is displayed in *Twopence Coloured* (1951), a collection that draws its sustenance chiefly from obscure sources in literature, painting, history, and sophisticated folk-lore. The component pieces, with their polished perfection of surface, their uniformity of style, and their variegated but elusive core of meaning, resemble nothing so closely as an array of crystal paper-weights. The interest of such a collection is necessarily confined in the main to fellow *bibeloteurs* who alone are qualified to determine the provenance and authenticity of the individual items. Hart-Smith is a more robust writer who has released in this country some of the large, loose freedom of Australian letters. No native poet, it is fairly safe to assert, would have ventured on a subject so gaping with pitfalls as that of *Christopher Columbus* (1948). Hart-Smith has skirted the obvious dangers by ignoring the legendary elements in the story and presenting it in a series of flat, laconic poems, verging at times on the prosaic. So successfully has he avoided the trap of romantic inflation that he has almost reduced the epic narrative to nullity: while his version is too sketchily episodic to rank as chronicle, its particularity deprives it of wider meaning. *On the Level* (1950) is a less ambitious work, containing impressions of Canterbury landscape and rural life, renderings of local legend, and other miscellaneous poems. Such modest and often perceptive verse has a documentary value in a district where writers have been few; besides which it has doubtless served the function of reconciling the poet himself to new surroundings. But how alien to the country is the free verse in which most of the impressions are presented—quite as alien to the native poetic genius as the Australian ballad metres so emphatically rejected in the past.

In its rural form, the native poetic genius has found its purest exponent in Ruth Dallas, lone poet of Southland. Her *Country Road* (1953) is as indigenous a work as *Tutira*, and in the same way the collection has grown from profound knowledge of a small area—a farming district (as revealed in the poems) of mountain, hill, and sea. This supplies the setting for the majority of the poems, the subject of some, and the source of a dual imagery of earth and sea that emerges often unexpectedly but always fittingly throughout the book. Despite her many felicities of observation, Ruth Dallas is no mere miniaturist of nature: the landscape, the shell, the bird is only the starting-point for meditations that move with a grave, slow cadence and seem to arise no less inevitably than the images from intimacy with earth and sea. Nature is neither hostile nor friendly in these poems: it has its existence apart from man, it is indifferent, and it is always changing. Transience is a recurring theme, and if there is a lesson it is one of acquiescence:

> *I shall be content with the watermarks on the sand,*
> *Experimental colours and casts of shells,*
> *The shapes of trees and time-worn rocks and hills,*
> *With all things carefully moulded, patterned or planned,*
> *And the rhythmical cycle of plants and seasons and lives*
> *That come and go like the tides, as slowly, as surely.*[24]

No poetry of recent times has shown at once equal fulfilment and equal promise.

The post-war record of imaginative prose has been in the main fragmentary and inconclusive—one of isolated first novels and collections, of scattered short stories, often of exceptional promise followed by silence. Indeed, posterity may find the enduring prose of the middle decades not in fiction but in writing where creative impulses are anchored to reality, where imagination is curbed by documents. Even to a contemporary and cursory eye the achievements of recent New Zealand scholarship make an impressive showing. The war itself inspired what is undoubtedly the most comprehensive scheme of research and publication yet attempted in this country: already the series of official histories has attained massive proportions and when completed will form not only a detailed account of the nation's war-time efforts but also a memorial to its late editor, Sir Howard Kippenberger. That rare combination of hero and scholar, of soldier and man of sensibility made his own contribution to the small library of memoirs that has emerged from the war. With its firmly disciplined prose, unfailing honesty, and leaven of laconic humour, *Infantry Brigadier* (1949) deserves to become a minor classic. Notable additions have also been made in less specialized branches of historical writing; among a number of examples, two may be cited: A. H. McLintock's *History of Otago* (1949), which is provincial only in scope, and Keith Sinclair's *Origins of the Maori Wars* (1957), a patient investigation into one of the most complex episodes of the past. Biography again has shown increasing technical skill and maturity of outlook. R. M. Burdon, local exponent of the brief life, has widened his range to produce in *King Dick* (1955) perhaps the first rounded portrait of a New Zealand statesman, while J. D. Pascoe's monumental *Mr. Explorer Douglas* (1957) presents in authentic terms that figure of national legend, the man alone. Finally (in a catalogue that cannot claim to be other than selective and superficial) reference must be made to *Katherine Mansfield* (1954). In that masterly work, where biographer and devotee meet in harmonious union, Antony Alpers revealed for the first time the inner recesses of Katherine Mansfield's life and discharged a debt to the unquiet spirit which has haunted New Zealand letters for two generations.

To attribute to Katherine Mansfield all the tendencies of recent New Zealand fiction would be to over-simplify a complex situation. The vogue of the short story, the cult of childhood, the painful concern with technique—for each of these many possible explanations may be found. Her example, reinforced by Sargeson's, does, however, appear to supply the main reason for the limited aims so characteristic of aspiring writers. In a literary environment as daunting as New Zealand's it is natural to lay aside larger ambitions and embrace the ideal of a petty perfectionism, especially when such a course is (or seems to be) sanctioned by the highest local precedent.

Whatever its source, the preoccupation with the small thing exquisitely done is well illustrated in two books of short stories published in 1957, Helen Shaw's *The Orange Tree* and Maurice Duggan's *Immanuel's Land*. Helen Shaw is a miniaturist of the past, a delineator of old customs, old houses, old men, above all of old women. She has a gift for suggesting an atmosphere of fusty decay, and her best effects are obtained by contrasting the remote with the present or decrepitude with youth. The strength of her work is in its detail, for she rarely produces a fully rounded, completely satisfying story. It is as if, having contrived her characters and created an atmosphere, she found herself at a loss to dispose of them. Hence a story that promises to lead to some macabre climax ends lamely as an anecdote whose point is obscured rather than revealed by a decorative symbolism. Duggan's collection, on the other hand, contains no adornments, no superfluities of expression. Means are perfectly adapted to ends, so that each story suggests that it has been hammered out by a tough but sensitive mind supremely aware of its purpose and sometimes over-conscious of its limitations. The approach ranges from a carefully controlled impressionism to a flexible realism (recalling the Joyce of *Dubliners*) employed in a striking group of stories set in a Catholic boarding-school. Here, after a period of experimentation, the writer seems to have found a method and perhaps a subject that encourage the highest expectations. Helen Shaw's sketches also show modest promise. But in illustrating the restrictive effects of the local environment, it must be emphasized that both these slim first collections are the work not of beginners but of writers who have been publishing for at least ten years.

Among serious post-war novelists none have been more successful in emancipating themselves from constricting ideals than two who have lived and worked abroad. Far removed from the preciosity of New Zealand circles, Dan Davin and James Courage have in little more than a decade achieved the impressive score of five books apiece. The detachment which has probably contributed to their fluency has brought its own consequences: their fiction is retrospective, sometimes nostalgic, based very often on memories of boyhood and youth. The effects of long expatriation are more marked in the older writer, Courage, whose settings are confined to the province of Canterbury and whose chronological limits rarely extend beyond the early nineteen-twenties. The small world he has conjured up so memorably is centred on the squattocracy, leading in their isolation a life which in externals has changed little since the nineteenth century. In the roomy homesteads where matrons dispense patronage and tea, electricity and wireless are unknown, servants are in attendance, and civilized standards are maintained in the face of a menacing colonialism. This society of the pastoral foot-hills is conducted, as the author remarks, 'in almost feudal style—England never forgotten'.[25] There is much coming and going between the two countries, and where the leading characters are not English-born, they are usually oriented towards the homeland. The unregenerate colonial appears either in an ancillary role or as a rough but robust foil to the 'English' characters. Courage's world is, in short, Lady Barker's, drained of its pioneer vigour and racked by neurotic desires which are frequently observed through the eyes of a precocious child.

In using his limited material, Courage displays a technical skill that bears traces of his apprenticeship to the drama. He is economical of both analysis and narrative, preferring to unfold his stories through a crisp dialogue which, at the crises of the plots, suggests—in the New Zealand context—an unlikely frankness in discussing the intimacies of emotional and sexual behaviour. The influence of the stage is most obvious in two of the slighter novels. *Fires in the Distance* (1952) and *The Call Home* (1956) resemble plays devised for a company with limited resources of scenery and actors. Both works provide a range of stock parts (including the wise white-haired *grande dame* and the infant prodigy), while in the former the action is so dramatically compressed as to become not merely implausible but ludicrous. *Desire without Content*

(1950) and *The Young Have Secrets* (1954) are more serious novels which make full use of devices proper to fiction and contain no stock characters. The two central figures—Mrs. Kendal in the first, Walter Blakiston in the second—are Courage's most complex studies of womanhood and childhood. The books are accomplished, eminently readable (as Courage always is), and, up to a point, convincing. But again one is conscious of the playwright manipulating his puppets and finally tying up the ends; so the total effect is macabre rather than tragic, poignant more than profound. To introduce such considerations is, however, to ignore Courage's implicit purpose; his intention is not to achieve 'greatness' but to give pleasure. In pursuing this modest but laudable aim he has, incidentally, anatomized a decaying society; and ever since the appearance of *The Fifth Child* (1948) he has shown to his sluggish compatriots an example of diligence combined always with a scrupulous concern for his craft.

Davin is a writer of larger scope and ambition whose settings include war-time Africa and post-war London but whose local territory is no more extensive—and hardly more typical—than the feudal domain of pastoral Canterbury. He rarely ventures north of Dunedin and confines himself for the most part to a spiritual enclave of the Southland province inhabited by Catholic families of Irish origin. The manners and morals of this little group, their religious beliefs, inherited grievances, and tenacious loyalties, have supplied the material for some of Davin's most successful fiction, and they are the recurring subject of contemplation from distant vantage points in Bloomsbury and Cairo. The community of devoted, pious women and hard-working, hard-drinking, back-sliding men was first presented in *Cliffs of Fall* (1945) through the critical eyes of Mark Burke who, with youthful arrogance, declares his interest in his 'own people' to be merely 'an academic one'.[26] For Mark is the embodiment of the ardent young colonial, resolved that no personal ties will restrain him from going overseas in pursuit of name and career. His removal of the chief obstacle to that ambition, the pathetic Marta, motivates the action of a powerful but improbable tale. In *Roads from Home* (1949) Davin dealt more sympathetically with his youthful *milieu* and widened his range to take in an entire family, the Hogans, together with a complicated clan of relatives and friends. The novel is, in effect, the vindication of a way of life, an affectionate tribute at the shrine of native pieties. Domestic tensions are analysed, scenes of violence introduced, but the final note is one of peaceful reconciliation: clan loyalties have been confirmed, and the Protestant daughter-in-law, who threatened family cohesion, has been summarily despatched. Both here and elsewhere, Davin dispenses justice to evil-doers as inexorably as did his southern predecessors, Bathgate and Ferguson.

Technically, Davin owes nothing to local precedent. He has adopted a Huxleyan conception of the novel, limited in plot and action, plentifully supplied with talk, and equipped with an interior monologue which acts as an infinitely expansible hold-all for the writer's reflections. In the restricted New Zealand settings the current of analysis and comment is comparatively restrained, but when stimulated by exotic scenes, it flows with copious abundance. Tony, one of the staff officers in *For the Rest of our Lives* (1947), remarks of his colleague Frank that he suffers from ' "the introspect's disease" '.[27] The complaint is common to all the major characters, growing most virulent in the feverish atmosphere of Cairo. Despite some meditative excesses and a weight of service terminology, the novel succeeds in giving a uniquely comprehensive picture of the New Zealand Division, that other clan to which Davin has pledged his allegiance. *The Sullen Bell* (1956) forms a kind of sequel to the war novel. In London are gathered assorted New Zealanders, dominated by veterans of the Division, who are shown making the transition from war to peace and in other ways releasing themselves from the past. This complex novel, in one of its aspects, completes a cycle that began with *Cliffs of Fall*. The expatriates have come to the metropolis not to seek some Jamesian ideal of the civilized life but, in the manner of Mark Burke, to carve out careers. Their pursuit of varied ambitions and unvarying diversions is related so circumstantially that certain passages seem to have strayed from the files of an exceptionally observant social historian. Indeed, only one of Davin's books is entirely free from a burden of social and political comment, his superb collection of short stories, *The Gorse Blooms Pale* (1947). There he ranges in differing moods over the scenes and periods covered by his longer fiction; and there, stripped of superfluities, his art is seen in its purest form.

The fluency of Courage and Davin has been equalled by two other novelists, Ruth Park and Guthrie Wilson, both working at a more popular level. Ruth Park is closely associated with Australia and should perhaps be relinquished to that province of letters. Her claim to local status rests on three books where the background is only too recognizably New Zealand—a land of Maoris, moas, spouting geysers, and snow-clad peaks—the New Zealand of the tourist brochure and nineteenth-century novel. Into this picturesque setting, with its eccentric and colourful population, there is invariably introduced a female waif whose vicissitudes provide a slender plot. Though the formula is constant, the treatment differs from work to work, ranging from the realistic-pathetic to the epic-historical. Ruth Park's not inconsiderable feat is to unite two art forms and two epochs, to suggest at once Mrs. Aylmer and Jennifer Jones. Wilson's later fiction also contains its cinematic promise. Even *Brave Company* (1951), in a heavily censored version, might be translated into an effective and serious film. That book has some claims to be considered the best war novel yet written by a New Zealander, certainly supplementing, if not surpassing, *For the Rest of our Lives*. Where Davin covers the whole Division in its African phase, Wilson concentrates on a few infantrymen in Italy, and he writes not from the officer's point of view but from the private soldier's. Rarely has life in the ranks been portrayed with such uncompromising directness. The novel seems to have come from some profound central experience to which the author repeatedly returns in his later fantasies of power and violence. In Brutto, the veteran who cannot recognize that the war is over, he has created in melodramatic terms a valid symbol, possibly failing to perceive its relevance to himself.

In an extravagant flight of fancy, Wilson has invented a New Zealander who at the age of fifty-one is the 'author of thirteen novels, four volumes of essays and many short stories'.[28] One may safely prophesy that no living writer will achieve that record (unless it be Wilson himself). Apart from the exceptions already mentioned, the younger novelists, whether working at home or abroad, have normally published one book, or at most two, and have then lapsed into silence. The resulting crop of fiction partly compensates in variety for what it lacks in bulk. It includes, for example, two works as dissimilar as *The Huntsman in his Career* (1949) by Erik de Mauny and *Voyagers in Aspic* (1954) by John Gillies. The former is that New Zealand rarity, a novel of ideas, based on a notorious war-time murder which the writer skilfully contrives to fit into the framework of Gallic theory. The analysis of the *acte gratuit* and its repercussions has supplied de Mauny with a neat device for assembling diverse characters and surveying with sympathetic insight a large area of society. Gillies is an innovator of a different sort who exploits the satirical possibilities of New Zealanders on the grand tour. His comic invention never falters as he pilots his cargo of dowagers, writers, *débutantes*, and adventurers through the intricacies of the English social scene. G. R. Gilbert is a third innovator. In *Glass-sharp and Poisonous* (1952) he has bravely attempted to climb the treacherous rock-face of allegory—with little more success, alas, than the woman whose fatal ascent forms one of his several centres of interest. This baffling and disappointing work shows neither the spontaneity nor the warmth of Gilbert's earlier sketches, *Free to Laugh and Dance* (1942), where the form was American but the content wholly indigenous. A similar combination is found in the most massive of these fictional monoliths, *The Cunninghams* (1948), David Ballantyne's masterly study of working-class family life in a New Zealand town. The book is of particular interest not merely for its intrinsic merits. Conceived in emulation of James T. Farrell, it bears the outward signs of his method—objectivity, colloquialness of style, lavishness in documentation. The result is, nevertheless, no amorphous piece of urban realism but a well-constructed novel, shaped very largely by local circumstances. The minutiae of small-town life are reproduced with the utmost fidelity, and from a crowded but representative cast there stands out that classical New Zealand tableau—the dominant, managing mother, flanked on one side by the diminished father, on the other by the sensitive, aspiring son. In the face of heavy odds, Ballantyne has achieved a triumph of literary adaptation.

The social interests of Ballantyne, combined in varying degrees with his formal accomplishments, are shared by three writers who have so far confined themselves to shorter flights of fiction. Douglas Stewart, the oldest of the trio, has stronger claims to New Zealand status in prose than in poetry. All the stories in his collection, *A Girl with Red Hair* (1944), have a local setting, often identifiable more specifically with Taranaki. He excels in retailing the humorous episode that is rich in character, laced with scandal, and most frequently aimed at official or pretentious personages—the typical product of a close-knit community of small towns and small farms. He has possibly found in Australia release from native inhibitions. His range is exceptionally wide, and he is free from moral or theoretical preoccupations; he reports but rarely comments and even more rarely reproves. Not so the New Zealand-based A. P. Gaskell—at least in the more complex stories of *The Big Game* (1947). There he condemns his reprobates —the possessive mother, the shallow schoolmistress, the weakly indulgent officer—and exposes the realities lying behind the front of 'the glorious party' or 'the devoted family'. Judgment and exposure never obtrude but arise as the characters take shape and the stories unfold. For the acuteness of Gaskell's moral sense is matched by the precision of his art. In using the colloquial monologue, he has learned from Sargeson, though he adapts the form to his own needs and employs other devices when they are more appropriate. His subjects are also allied to Sargeson's. As Robert Chapman has shown in 'Fiction and the Social Pattern' (*Landfall*, March 1953), Gaskell is the authority on the peculiarly male reserve enclosed within the barriers of the football 'gym', the 'boozer', and the military camp. The third writer, John Reece Cole, has claimed for himself another distinctive province of fiction: he is the chronicler of that legion of youthful New Zealanders who served, scattered war-time exiles, in units of the Royal Air Force. If the service stories of *It Was so Late* (1949) were arranged in chronological sequence, they would form a fairly complete and singularly sensitive record of experience common to many in the writer's generation. Combined with this cycle is a later group which handles peacetime themes and suggests that, having expressed a sombre episode in his life, Cole then resolutely inscribed 'finis'. In the post-war stories, he proves himself a keen observer of the urban middle class, acutely aware of its unacknowledged gradations, as also of the conflicts to which they frequently give rise. The elements of an original novel are latent in 'A Touch of the Old Trouble'—an observation that also applies to Gaskell's 'Holiday' and to the title story of Stewart's collection. For all three writers possess serious and substantial talents which on occasion chafe at the limitations of the short story. They may at present be engaged on work of ampler scale; but the years pass, and the novels, the *contes*, even the further collections of stories, fail to appear.

Until the explosive publication of *Owls Do Cry* in 1957, Janet Frame would have found a place among the authors of first and only collections, or she might have stood alone as a feminine miniaturist of exceptional originality. Nothing quite resembling *The Lagoon* (1951) had previously been seen in this country. Childhood reminiscences, character sketches, glimpses of city life, strange episodes that crossed the border into fantasy—all were presented in a free, colloquial, intimate prose and developed by an ostensibly casual method of association. Viewed in the perspective of present knowledge, the stories and sketches disclose many features of the novel, including some of its major themes; what they fail to hint at is the writer's later capacity to organize into a harmonious whole an immense, intractable mass of human experience and physical detail. *Owls Do Cry* gives imaginative form not merely to a family, the Withers, but to an entire town, Waimaru; and Janet Frame has accomplished this feat of synthesis while discarding the structural props of conventional fiction. In their place she has used an elaborate—perhaps over-elaborate— system of recurring themes, symbolic cross-references, echoing words and phrases, so that the work resembles an intricate poem rather than a novel in the usually accepted sense. As always, technique is significant for what it achieves, and Janet Frame's innovations are mentioned merely because they—and her 'poetic' methods in general—enable her to evoke objects and people with an immediacy that imparts to them almost palpable existence. The children picking over treasure in the rubbish dump, Amy Withers buttering up her menfolk, the mental patients in their festal gyrations—these and numerous other episodes, once read, remain etched upon the mind. The book inevitably has its 'faults', of which the most serious is the perfunctory rendering of that central incident, Francie's death. In the long run, however, Janet Frame's 'faults' matter as little as, say, Dostoevsky's. One goes to such writers not in search of the flawless trifle but to be exalted for a time to their plane of perception and to follow their lead into secret places of the spirit.

That Janet Frame is not alone in having found release from inhibiting preconceptions has become evident only as the writing of this essay has drawn to a close. By way of postscript and conclusion reference must be made to three books published in the early months of 1958. Each is a first novel, each in its own way opens up new imaginative territory, and each, it seems probable, will ultimately have a place in the canon of serious New Zealand fiction. Sylvia Ashton-Warner has entered the schoolroom for the substance of her *Spinster*, a loose, rich, rhapsodic work that owes nothing to precedent, European or local. Breaking with convention quite as decisively as Janet Frame, she has abandoned such devices as narrative to present the small world of school and *pa* solely through the sensibility of her title figure, Anna Vorontosov. In this brandy-swigging, flower-communing, 'phantasy'-spinning infant-mistress, the author has created a highly original—if sometimes extravagantly implausible—character; but her greatest triumph is the evocation in all its fruitful anarchy of the 'pre-fab', battlefield of races, theories, personalities. The scene of M. K. Joseph's *I'll Soldier No More* is also a battlefield—rather, a succession of battlefields—but in no figurative sense. An accomplished poet here proves himself an exponent of the prose virtues, master of a clean, flexible narrative style, while sensitively attuned to the nuances of spoken idiom. No previous war novel has been more carefully plotted, none more conscientiously documented, none in the balance between waiting and action, boredom and danger more forcefully conveys the impression of complete authenticity. With Ian Cross's *The God Boy* (first published the previous year in the United States) the scene is again the familiar one of the New Zealand small town. The seaside village of Raggleton is convincingly presented through the eyes of the child narrator, but the setting figures far less prominently than it did in *The Cunninghams* or even in *Owls Do Cry*. The interest of this profound and economical little novel is concentrated on the uncompromising theologian, Jimmy Sullivan, caught up in the bewildering complications of adult passion. Not only does *The God Boy* transcend the social interests of the thirties, it goes beyond the category of the psychological to introduce into New Zealand literature what is perhaps its first genuine note of tragedy.

The appearance within a few months of four novels of marked distinction lightens an otherwise drab period and justifies a concluding note of mild optimism. This sign of renewed vitality does little, however, to modify the general pattern of New Zealand's literary development over the past decades. As one glances back to the thirties, it would be idle to suggest that there yet exists any well-defined, firmly established tradition of local fiction. The picture is still predominantly one of individual achievement and isolated experiment. The poetic record—conveniently presented in Robert Chapman and Jonathan Bennett's *Anthology of New Zealand Verse* (1956)—differs slightly: among certain southern poets in particular resemblances are sometimes discernible between writer and writer or between generation and generation. But the links are tenuous and may indicate temperamental or social affinities as much as common literary aims. Louis Johnson's 'poetic Crusoes' conforms more closely to the facts than the notion of a unified 'school'. What is apparent through the welter of independent effort in prose and poetry is a growing tradition of craftsmanship and, more significantly, the emergence of a distinctive outlook, humanistic, compassionate, somewhat sceptical. In these islands and with increasing frequency beyond their limits a new accent is becoming audible, the native accent of New Zealand.

REFERENCES TO QUOTATIONS

I.

Before the Colonists

1. John Ogilby, *America* (London, 1671), p. 655.
2. Robert Hooke, *Philosophical Collections* (London), No. 6, March 1682, pp. 180–2.
3. *An Account of the Discoveries Made in the South Pacific Ocean* (London, 1767), p. 102.
4. *An Historical Collection of the Several Voyages and Discoveries in the South Pacific Ocean* (London, 1770–1), I, p. xxviii.
5. *An Account of the Voyages Undertaken . . . for Making Discoveries in the Southern Hemisphere* (London, 1773), II, p. 284.
6. Ibid., p. 341.
7. *A Journal of a Voyage to the South Seas* (London, 1773), pp. 122, 97.
8. *Voyage round the World* (London, 1777), I, p. 148.
9. Loc. cit.
10. *Voyage round the World*, I, p. 179.
11. Hawkesworth, II, p. 314; Parkinson, p. 88.
12. *Journal of Captain Cook's Last Voyage* (London, 1781), p. 73.
13. *Voyage round the World*, I, p. 517.
14. *A Voyage towards the South Pole* (London, 1777), I, p. 245.
15. Ibid., p. 130.
16. *Nouveau Voyage à la Mer du Sud* (Paris, 1783), pp. 95, 128.
17. Ibid., pp. 125, 145, 146.
18. M. de Rossel (ed.), *Voyage de Dentrecasteaux* (Paris, 1808), pp. 271–2.
19. *Voyage de la Corvette l'Astrolabe* (Paris, 1830–5), II, pp. 10–11, 32, 115–16; see Wright, *New Zealand 1826–1827* (Wellington, 1950), pp. 66–67, 79, 127–8.
20. *Voyage de l'Astrolabe*, III, p. 2; Wright, *New Zealand*, p. 26.

REFERENCES TO QUOTATIONS

21. *Voyage au Pole Sud* (Paris, 1841–6), IX, p. 126; see Wright, *The Voyage of the 'Astrolabe'—1840* (Wellington, 1955), pp. 17–18.
22. *Some Account of New Zealand* (London, 1807), pp. 3, 16.
23. *Journal of a Ten Months' Residence in New Zealand* (London, 1823), p. 253.
24. *Narrative of a Voyage to New Zealand* (London, 1817), I, pp. 86, 337.
25. J. R. Elder (ed.), *The Letters and Journals of Samuel Marsden* (Dunedin, 1932), pp. 122, 129.
26. Ibid., pp. 60, 61.
27. *A Narrative of a Nine Months' Residence in New Zealand* (London, 1832), pp. 39, 58, 138, 65.

II.

Colonial Beginnings

1. *Poetical Works* (London, n.d.), p. 213.
2. *Poems of Arthur Hugh Clough* (London, 1909), p. 256.
3. *Venice* (London, 1839), p. 27.
4. *Canterbury Papers* (London, 1850–2), p. 115.
5. W. F. Alexander and A. E. Currie (eds.), *New Zealand Verse* (London, 1906), p. 4.
6. Province of Canterbury, New Zealand, *Journal of Proceedings of the Provincial Council* (Christchurch, 1864), p. 10.
7. *Letters to J. E. FitzGerald* (typescript, Alexander Turnbull Library), p. 117, letter of 31 May 1892.

III.

Seminal Years

1. *Chapman's New Zealand Monthly Magazine* (Auckland), August 1862, p. 3.
2. *Adventure in New Zealand* (London, 1845), I, pp. 17–18.
3. Ibid., pp. 319, 151, 144, II, pp. 4, 30, 222.
4. Ibid., I, p. 299.
5. Ibid., pp. 44–45.
6. *Travels in New Zealand* (London, 1843), I, pp. 37, 41–42.

7. Ibid., pp. 365, 359, II, pp. 138, 137.
8. Ibid., I, pp. 383, 416–17, II, p. 153.
9. *Savage Life and Scenes* (London, 1847), I, p. 224.
10. Ibid., I, p. 267, II, p. 2, I, p. 338.
11. *Maori Religion and Mythology* (London, 1882), p. vii.
12. *Traditions and Superstitions of the New Zealanders* (London, 1854), p. 196.
13. Ibid., p. v.
14. *Te Ika a Maui* (London, 1855), p. 55.
15. *Polynesian Mythology* (London, 1855), pp. 58, 124, 134, 159–60, 149.
16. Ibid., pp. ix, xi, xiii.
17. *The Story of New Zealand* (London, 1859), I, pp. iii, 5, II, pp. 188, 279, 314, 309.
18. Ibid., I, p. iv.
19. T. M. Hocken, *Contributions to the Early History of New Zealand* (London, 1898), p. 201.
20. *Martin's Locals* (Christchurch, 1862), pp. 23, 25, 26.
21. *The Book of Canterbury Rhymes* (Christchurch, 1866), pp. 39–40.
22. Ibid., p. 84.
23. *New Zealander* (Auckland), 13 September 1851.
24. W. F. Alexander and A. E. Currie (eds.), *A Treasury of New Zealand Verse* (Auckland, etc., 1926), p. 7.
25. *New Zealander*, 1 May 1847.
26. 10 July 1852.
27. 19 November 1853.
28. *The Pigeons' Parliament* (Wellington, 1854), pp. 58, 33.
29. *Poems and Songs* (Edinburgh, 1861), pp. 46, 158, 149.
30. *Land of the Morning* (Christchurch, 1909), p. 36.

IV.

The Period of Expansion

1. *A First Year in Canterbury Settlement* (London, 1863), p. 51.
2. Ibid., pp. 60, 65, 69, 70–71.
3. Ibid., p. 51.

4. *Station Life in New Zealand* (London, 1870), p. 105.
5. *Distant Homes* (London, 1862), pp. 32, 71, 199.
6. *Station Amusements in New Zealand* (London, 1873), p. 103.
7. *Over the Hills and Far Away* (London, 1874), p. vi; *A Strange Friendship* (London, 1874), pp. 30, 105–6, 94.
8. *A Strange Friendship*, pp. 112, 2, 14, 13, 31.
9. J. H. K., *Henry Ancrum* (London, 1872), I, p. [v].
10. Dugald Ferguson, *Vicissitudes of Bush Life in Australia and New Zealand* (London, 1891), p. 17; *Mates* (London, 1911), p. 375.
11. *The Narrative of Edward Crewe* (London, 1874), pp. iii, 4, 284.
12. *Bush Life*, p. 284, *Mates*, p. 378, *Bush Life*, p. 261.
13. *Edward Crewe*, p. 17.
14. *A Rolling Stone* (London, 1886), I, p. 86.
15. *Philosopher Dick* (London, 1891), p. 228.
16. Ibid., pp. 87, 99, 100, 112–13.
17. Ibid., pp. 165, 440, 369.
18. *The Maori King* (London, 1864), pp. 145–6, 243.
19. *Reminiscences of the War in New Zealand* (London, 1879), pp. viii, 12, 95, 206.
20. R. P. Whitworth, *Hine-Ra* (Melbourne, 1887), p. 21.
21. *Henry Ancrum*, I, p. 147.
22. *Poenamo* (London, 1881), pp. v, 38, 328.
23. *Old New Zealand* (Auckland, 1863), p. 1.
24. Ibid., p. 202.
25. Ibid., pp. 142–3, 217.
26. Ibid. (London, 1876), p. xix.
27. *Wild Will Enderby* (London, 1873), p. 70.
28. *Frank Melton's Luck* (Auckland, 1891), p. 2.
29. *Anno Domini 2000* (London, 1889), pp. 28–29.
30. Ibid., p. 31.
31. Ibid., p. 28.
32. *Transactions and Proceedings of the New Zealand Institute* (Wellington, 1870), II, p. 264.
33. *Poems and Sketches* (London, n.d.), pp. 85–86.
34. *Poems* (Christchurch, 1861), p. 9.

35. *The Monthly Review* (Wellington), May 1890, p. 280.
36. *Poems from New Zealand* (London, 1868), p. 114.
37. *Passages in a Wandering Life* (London, 1900), p. 7.
38. *Ranolf and Amohia* (2nd. ed., London, 1883), I, p. viii.
39. Ibid., p. 5.
40. Ibid., II, pp. 243-4.
41. *Paddy Murphy's Budget* (Dunedin, 1880), pp. 60, 5.
42. *Behind the Tomb* (Melbourne, 1871), p. 7.
43. *Lays of the Land of the Maori and Moa* (London, 1884), p. 126.
44. *Colonial Couplets* (Christchurch, 1889), p. 3.

v.

The Nineties

1. *Democracy in New Zealand*, tr. E. V. Burns (London, 1914), p. 271.
2. *New Zealand Illustrated Magazine* (Auckland), October 1899, p. 2.
3. *Democracy in New Zealand*, p. 97.
4. Alexander and Currie, *Treasury of New Zealand Verse*, pp. 1-2.
5. *The Passing of the Forest* (London, 1925), p. 13.
6. *Democracy in New Zealand*, p. 97.
7. *The Spirit of the Rangatira* (Melbourne, 1889), p. v.
8. Ibid., p. 35.
9. *The Sitter on the Rail* (Christchurch, 1891), p. 24.
10. *Literature and Authorship in New Zealand* (London, 1943), p. 19.
11. *Land of the Morning* (Christchurch, 1909), p. 130.
12. *A Knight of the Holy Ghost* (London, 1907), pp. [ii], 176.
13. *In Revolt* (London, 1893), p. 186.
14. *Vigil* (Auckland, etc., 1935), p. 6.
15. *Ko Meri* (London, 1890), pp. 307, 29, 53, 61.
16. Ibid., pp. 133, 179, 394.
17. Ibid., p. 389.
18. *Alice Lauder* (London, 1893), p. 190.
19. *Two Summers* (London, 1900), p. 21.
20. *Alice Lauder*, p. 130.

21. *Two Summers*, pp. 153, 174, 195.
22. *New Zealand Illustrated Magazine*, October 1900, p. 84.
23. Ibid., October 1899, pp. 1–2.

VI.
Years of Prosperity

1. *The Heart of the Bush* (London, 1910), pp. 46–47, 45, 87.
2. Ibid., pp. 281, 124, 281.
3. *The Elixir of Life* (London, 1907), p. 4.
4. *Australia and New Zealand* (London, 1873), II, p. 457.
5. *Home* (London, 1927), p. 8.
6. Isabel M. Cluett, *Waif's Progress* (London, 1929), p. [4].
7. John Middleton Murry (ed.), *The Letters of Katherine Mansfield* (London, 1928), II, p. 199.
8. Ruth Elvish Mantz and J. Middleton Murry, *The Life of Katherine Mansfield* (London, 1933), p. 43.
9. Ibid., pp. 260, 266, 283.
10. *In a German Pension* (London, 1911), pp. 144, 137.
11. Mantz and Murry, pp. 326, 327.
12. J. Middleton Murry (ed.), *Journal of Katherine Mansfield* (London, 1927), pp. ix–x.
13. Letters, II, p. 196.
14. Ibid.
15. *Katherine Mansfield* (Auckland, 1936), p. 1.
16. *Journal*, p. 42.
17. *Brown Bread from a Colonial Oven* (London, 1912), p. 140.
18. *The Toll of the Bush* (London, 1905), p. 119.
19. *The Story of a New Zealand River* (London, 1920), p. 31.
20. *Allen Adair* (London, 1925), p. 11.
21. *Novels and Novelists* (London, 1930), p. 219.
22. *Follow the Call* (Dunedin, 1936), p. 8.
23. Frank S. Anthony and Francis Jackson, *Me and Gus* (Wellington, 1951), p. 6.
24. *Tutira* (Edinburgh and London, 1921), pp. vi, 8.

25. Ibid., pp. viii, 133.
26. Ibid., pp. 121, 265, 292.
27. Ibid., pp. 147, 400.
28. *Sorrows and Joys of a New Zealand Naturalist* (Dunedin, 1936), p. 16.
29. *Shingle Short* (Christchurch, 1908), p. 11.
30. Ibid., p. 58.
31. Quentin Pope (ed.), *Kowhai Gold* (London, 1930), p. 110.
32. *Golden Wedding* (London, 1932), p. 17.
33. *Poems* (Dunedin, 1921), p. 13.
34. *New Zealand Bird Songs* (Wellington, 1929), p. [9].
35. *Poems* (London, 1937), pp. 31, 48, 18.
36. *More Poems* (London, 1951), pp. 7, 57, 68.
37. Ibid., p. 45.

VII.

The Thirties

1. *Phoenix* (Auckland), March 1932, pp. [4], [5].
2. Ibid., July 1932, pp. 34, 37.
3. *He Shall Not Rise* (London, 1930), p. 27.
4. Ibid., p. 85.
5. *Art in New Zealand* (Wellington), June 1934, pp. 213–18.
6. *He Shall Not Rise*, p. 14.
7. *Strange Rendezvous* (Christchurch, 1952), p. 57.
8. Ibid., p. 11.
9. *Three Poems* (Wellington, 1952), pp. 67, 50.
10. Ibid., p. 64.
11. *The Beggar* (Auckland, 1924), p. 3.
12. Ibid., p. 17.
13. Ibid., p. 15.
14. *No New Thing* (Auckland, 1934), p. xxv.
15. Ibid., p. i.
16. *End of Day* (Christchurch, 1936), p. [10].
17. *Not in Narrow Seas* (Christchurch, 1939), p. [9].
18. *Island and Time* (Christchurch, 1941), p. 12.
19. Ibid, p. 31.

REFERENCES TO QUOTATIONS

20. *The Wind and the Sand* (Christchurch, 1945), p. 14.
21. *13 Poems* (Christchurch, 1939), p. 1.
22. *The Wind and the Sand*, p. 38.
23. *Arawata Bill* (Christchurch, 1952), p. 38.
24. *Selected Poems* (Christchurch, 1940), p. 15.
25. *She Was my Spring* (Christchurch, 1954), p. 28.
26. *From a Garden in the Antipodes* (London, 1929), p. 16.
27. *Collected Poems* (Christchurch, 1950), p. 12.
28. Ibid., p. 52.
29. Ibid., p. 95.
30. *Houses by the Sea* (Christchurch, 1952), p. 122.
31. Ibid, p. 126.
32. *Art in New Zealand*, June 1934, p. 216.
33. *Poems 1921–1927* (London, 1928), p. 63.
34. July 1932, p. 23.
35. *The Godwits Fly* (London, 1938), pp. 52, 7.
36. *T'ien Hsia Monthly*, August 1938, p. 23.
37. *Report on Experience* (London, 1947), pp. 17, 2, 3, 2, 4, 15.
38. Ibid., p. 5.
39. *Man Alone* (London, 1939), p. 254.
40. *Brown Man's Burden* (Auckland, 1938), p. [ix].
41. *Discovered Isles* (Christchurch, 1950), p. 12.

VIII.
The Middle Decades

1. *Discovered Isles*, p. 190.
2. *The Quest* (London, 1946), pp. 7, 42.
3. *The Land and the People* (Christchurch, 1939), p. 23.
4. *The Estate* (Christchurch, 1957), p. 10.
5. *New Zealand Poetry Yearbook*, I (Wellington, 1951), p. 65, II (1952), p. 7, III (1953), p. 7.
6. *The Sun among the Ruins* (Christchurch, 1951), p. 49.
7. *Recent Trends in New Zealand Poetry* (Christchurch, 1951), pp. 17, 18.

8. *The Fallen House* (Christchurch, 1953), pp. 17, 14, 15.
9. *Mine Eyes Dazzle* (Christchurch, 1950), p. 13.
10. *The Bright Sea* (Christchurch, 1951), p. 9.
11. *Recent Trends*, p. 9.
12. *Fire without Phoenix* (Christchurch, 1957), p. 25.
13. *The Falcon Mask* (Christchurch, 1951), pp. 7, 14.
14. *Shadow of the Flame* (Auckland, 1950), p. 8.
15. Ibid., pp. 16, 26, 32; *The Falcon Mask*, pp. 9, 19, 21.
16. *Fire without Phoenix*, pp. 9, 24.
17. Ibid., p. 37.
18. *Imaginary Islands* (Auckland, 1950), p. 13.
19. *Strangers or Beasts* (Christchurch, 1954), p. 13.
20. *The Blind Mountain* (Christchurch, 1950), p. 9.
21. *Starveling Year* (Christchurch, 1953), p. 29.
22. Ibid., p. 20.
23. *Canterbury* (Christchurch, 1949), pp. 26, 32.
24. *Country Road* (Christchurch, 1953), p. 23.
25. *Desire without Content* (London, 1950), p. 18.
26. *Cliffs of Fall* (London, 1945), p. 40.
27. *For the Rest of our Lives* (London, 1947), p. 149.
28. *Sweet White Wine* (London, 1956), p. 6.

Index

Adams, Arthur H. (1872–1936), 80
Alpers, Antony (b. 1919), 151
Andersen, Johannes C. (b. 1873), 80
Angas, George French (1822–86), 26–27
Anthony, Frank S. (1891–1925), 96–97
Arachne, 139
Arena, 137
Art in New Zealand, 110, 121, 137
Arts Year Book, 137
Ashton-Warner, Sylvia, 160
Aylmer, Mrs. J. E., 42–43, 156

B(aines), W. M. (?–1912), 46–47, 48–49
Ballantyne, David (b. 1924), 157–8, 161
Barker, Lady Mary Anne (1831–1911), quoted, 42; her writings, 43–44; elsewhere mentioned, 49, 65, 153
Barr, John (1809–89), mentioned, 22; as entertainer, 33; his verse, 37–39
Barry, W. J. (1819–1907), 61
Bathgate, Alexander (1845–1930), 47, 59, 155
Baucke, William (1848–1931), 94
Baughan, B. E. (1870–1958), 91–92, 104
Baxter, James K. (b. 1926), 120, 141–2, 144, 145
Beaglehole, J. C. (b. 1901), 6, 117, 121
Bennett, Jonathan (b. 1930), 161
Bertram, James (b. 1910), 108
Best, Elsdon (1856–1931), 80, 98, 99
Bethell, Mary Ursula (1874–1945), 122–3, 135, 149
Bowen, Sir C. C. (1830–1917), 64, 103
Bracken, Thomas (1843–98), 67–68
Brasch, Charles (b. 1909), 137–9, 141
Broome, Sir Frederick Napier (1842–96), 65
Buick, T. Lindsay (1866–1938), 98
Burdon, R. M. (b. 1896), 151
Burn, D. W. M. (1862–1951), 65
Butler, Samuel (1835–1902), 40–41, 50, 64

Campbell, Alistair (b. 1926), 143

Campbell, Sir John Logan (1817–1912), 55–56
Campbell, Thomas, quoted, 16
Chamier, George, 50–52, 59, 75, 130
Chapman, Robert (b. 1922), 158, 161
Cheeseman, Clara (1852–1943), 49
Clough, Arthur Hugh, quoted, 16
Cole, John Reece (b. 1916), 158–9
Condliffe, J. B. (b. 1891), 84
Cook, Captain James (1728–79), accounts of expeditions, 3–7; elsewhere mentioned, 8, 9, 10, 12, 102
Cottle, Thos. (1845?–1923), 60–61
Courage, James (b. 1905), 152–4, 156
Cowan, James (1870–1943), 80
Cresswell, Walter D'Arcy (b. 1896), 124–126, 130, 135
Cross, Ian (b. 1925), 161
Crozet, Julien (1728–80), 7–8
Cruise, Richard (1784?–1832), 11
Curnow, Allen (b. 1911), his verse, 117–18, 120; as anthologist, 136–7, 141; elsewhere mentioned, 140

Dallas, Ruth (b. 1919), 150
Dalrymple, Alexander (1737–1808), 3
Davidson, William (1847–1912), 60
Davin, Dan (b. 1913), 152, 154–6
de Mauny, Erik (b. 1918), 157
Devanny, Jean, 96
Dieffenbach, Ernest (1811–55), 24–26, 27 101
Domett, Alfred (1811–87), quoted, 17; as colonist, 19, 22; his verse, 65–67, 103
Dowling, Basil (b. 1910), 148
Doyle, Charles (b. 1928), 145
Duggan, Eileen, 105–7, 120
Duggan, Maurice (b. 1922), 152
Dumont d'Urville, J. S. C. (1790–1842), accounts of expeditions, 8–10; elsewhere mentioned, 31

Earle, Augustus (1798–?), 13–14, 27

INDEX

Elder, J. R. (b. 1880), 12
Evans, Mrs. C. (1842?–82), 44–46

Fairburn, A. R. D. (1904–57), his verse, 110–14, 120; on Cresswell, 124; and John Mulgan, 129; and Brasch, 139; and Johnson, 141
Farjeon, B. L. (1838–1903), 59, 60, 84
Ferguson, Dugald (1833–1920), quoted, 46; his fiction, 47–48, 59; on poetry, 64; elsewhere mentioned, 155
Fiction, pioneer, 42–52 *passim*; Maori war, 54–55; gold-mining, 59–63 *passim*; of nineties, 73–79 *passim*; of 1900–1930, 86–97; of thirties, 126–34; contemporary, 151–61
Finlayson, Roderick (b. 1904), 130–2
FitzGerald, James Edward (1818–96), as representative colonist, 18–19, 22; and Butler, 40; and Chamier, 50; and Vogel, 63–64, 83
Forster, George (1754–94), 4–5, 11, 12
Frame, Janet (b. 1924), 159–60, 161
France, Ruth, *see* Henderson, Paul

Gaskell, A. P. (b. 1913), 158, 159
Gilbert, G. R. (b. 1917), 157
Gilbert, Ruth (b. 1917), 142–3
Gillies, John (b. 1920), 157
Glover, Denis (b. 1912), as typographer, 110; his verse, 117, 118–20; and Lee, 127; and John Mulgan, 130; and Brasch, 139
Golder, William (1810–76), 35–37
Gorst, Sir J. E. (1835–1916), 53, 54, 57
Grace, A. A. (1867–1942), 77
Grey, Sir George (1812–98), quoted, 19; his Maori collections, 28–30, 58; and Satchell, 94; elsewhere mentioned, 22
Grossmann, Edith Searle (1863–1931), her fiction, 73–75, 82–83; and Jane Mander, 94; elsewhere mentioned, 107, 126
Gudgeon, T. W. (1816–90), 53–54
Guthrie-Smith, W. H. (1861–1940), his writings, 98–102; elsewhere mentioned, 84, 104, 150

Haelbos, Henrick, 2
Hamilton, Augustus (1853–1913), 77
Hart-Smith, W. (b. 1911), 148, 149–50
Hawkesworth, John (1715?–73), 3–6 *passim*, 11
Heeres, J. E. (1858–1932), 3
Henderson, Paul (b. 1913), 148–9

Here and Now, 139
Hervey, J. R. (1889–1958), 121–2
Hight, Sir James (1872–1958), 80
Hilltop, 139
Hocken, T. M. (1836–1910), 33
Holcroft, M. H. (b. 1902), 134–5, 137, 140
Hume, Fergus (1859–1932), 84
Hyde, Robin (1906–39), her verse, 123–4; her fiction, 127–9; elsewhere mentioned, 89, 143

Inglewood, Kathleen (b. 1876), 75
Isitt, Kate Evelyn, *see* Inglewood, Kathleen

Johnson, Louis (b. 1924), 139–41, 142, 161
Joseph, M. K. (b. 1914), 145–6, 160–1

K., J. H., 46, 55
Kippenberger, Sir Howard (1897–1957), 151

Landfall, 137, 138, 139, 143, 146, 158
Lapham, Henry (1852?–87), 60
Lee, John A. (b. 1891), 126–7, 130
Lowry, R. W. (b. 1912), 110

Mackay, Jessie (1864–1938), as vernacular poet, 38; her verse, 71–73, 75, 77, 80, 81, 103; and Eileen Duggan, 105, 106
McLintock, A. H. (b. 1903), 151
Mander, Jane (1877–1949), 94–96, 126
Maning, F. E. (1811–83), 55, 56–59
Mansfield, Katherine (1888–1923), her literary development, 86–91; and Jane Mander, 95, 96; and Robin Hyde, 124; her biography, 151; elsewhere mentioned, 84, 92, 108
Marsden, Samuel (1765–1838), 11, 12–13
Martin, C. J. (1839?–1906), 33
Mason, R. A. K. (b. 1905), as editor, 108–109; his verse, 111, 114–17, 120; and Curnow, 117; and Johnson, 141
Mulgan, Alan (b. 1881), and Jessie Mackay, 73; his *Home*, 85; his verse, 105, 120–1
Mulgan, John (1911–45), 129–30

New Zealand Company, 1, 22, 23–24, 25, 35, 41
New Zealand Illustrated Magazine, 70, 79–80
New Zealand Listener, 137
New Zealand New Writing, 137
New Zealand Poetry Yearbook, 139–40
Nicholas, John Liddiard, 11–12

INDEX

Nierop, Dirck Rembrantszoon van (1610–1682), 2–3
Numbers, 139

Oliver, W. H. (b. 1925), 144–5

Park, Ruth, 156
Parkinson, Sydney (1745?–71), 4, 5, 7
Pascoe, J. D. (b. 1908), 151
Phoenix, 108–10, 117, 137, 139
Polack, Joel Samuel (1807–82), 14
Pyke, Vincent (1827–94), 59–60

Raven, Sarah (?–1868), 33
Rawlinson, Gloria (b. 1918), 123, 145, 147–8
Reeves, William Pember (1857–1932), as humorous versifier, 68; his writings, 70–71, 80, 103; elsewhere mentioned, 73, 81, 105
Rickman, John, 5, 6
Rochon, Alexis (1741–1817), 8
Rouse, J. T. (1832–84), 34

Sargeson, Frank (b. 1903), his fiction, 132–134; and Brasch, 139; and Gaskell, 158; elsewhere mentioned, 92, 151
Satchell, William (1860–1942), 84, 92–94
Savage, John (1770–1838), 11
Scholefield, Guy H. (b. 1877), 80
Schwimmer, Erik (b. 1923), 140
Sewell, Arthur (b. 1903), 91
Shaw, Helen (b. 1913), 152
Shortland, Edward (1812–93), 27–28, 30, 31, 58
Siegfried, André (b. 1875), 69, 70, 74, 78, 84
Simpson, Helen M. (b. 1890), 122
Sinclair, Keith (b. 1922), 145, 146, 151
Smith, S. Percy (1840–1922), 98
Smithyman, Kendrick (b. 1922), 145, 146–147

Spear, Charles (b. 1910), 148, 149
Stanley, Mary (b. 1919), 145, 147
Stevens, Joan (b. 1908), 56
Stewart, Douglas (b. 1913), 158, 159
Stoney, B. (1816–94), 54

Tasman, Abel Janszoon (1603?–59), accounts of expedition, 2–3; elsewhere mentioned, 3, 6, 7, 9, 102
Taylor, Richard (1805–73), 28
Thomson, Arthur S. (1816–60), 30–31, 32, 40
Tombs, Harry H. (b. 1874), 137
Tomorrow, 110, 132, 137
Trollope, Anthony, quoted, 85
Tupper, Martin, quoted, 18

Valentyn, François (1666–1727), 3
Verse, emigrant, 18–19; of 1840–60, 32–39; of 1860–90, 64–68; of nineties, 70–73, 75; of 1900–30, 102–7; of thirties, 110–126; contemporary, 137–50
Vogel, Harry B. (1868–1947), 77
Vogel, Sir Julius (1835–99), 39, 61–63, 69, 83
Vogt, Anton (b. 1914), 142

Wakefield, Edward Jerningham (1820–1879), 22–24, 25, 26, 31
Watson, H. B. M. (1863–1921), 55
Webb, Alice F. (b. 1876), 91–92
Weston, Jessie, 75–77
White, John (1826–91), 55, 66, 94
Williams, G. P. (1847–1909), 68
Wilson, Anne Glenny (1848–1930), 75, 78–79
Wilson, George H. (1833–1905), 55, 66, 94
Wilson, Guthrie (b. 1914), 156–7
Wilson, Pat (b. 1926), 143
Witheford, Hubert (b. 1921), 144
Witsen, Nicolaes (1641–1717), 3
Wright, Olive (b. 1886), 8